EXHIBITION DESIGN

daab

Architects/Designers	Project	
Introduction		

INTRODUCTION

Over the past fifty years, many of the innovations that have been implemented in architecture and interior design would never have seen the light of day, or would at least have taken much longer to appear if it hadn't been for the fertile testing ground of portable architecture. There has barely been an important architect in the world for the past century that has not taken advantage of the possibilities of the tentative play and experimentation provided by the design of exhibition sites for trade fairs and world expos. In fact, this branch of architecture includes milestones such as Alvar Aalto's Finnish Pavilion for the Venice Biennale and the German Pavilion of the 1929 Barcelona World Exposition, and such is the importance of these two examples of portable architecture that they are both still standing today. If the great designers often turn to this type of work it is because it embodies an intermediate step between the creation of marquees and the construction of large buildings, and this gives flight to their creativity.

The design of exhibition spaces also entails a number of added difficulties which can turn into real challenges for their creators, such as budgetary limitations, lack of space and the proverbial need for structures that can be quickly installed and easily disassembled by small teams of workers. This circumstance often leads people to view this branch of architecture as a game.

This publication aims to provide a balanced combination of very recent examples from trade fairs and cultural installations. The differences between the two are obvious, as the former aim for optimal product positioning to promote sales, while the latter work on the best way to publicize ideas, information or works of art.

The spectacular selection of projects in this book ranges from a small stand designed to capture the visitor's attention at a large trade fair, such as the Sci Fi project, to large exhibition sites of museum-like proportion such as the BMW Pavilion, as well as temporary exhibition spaces in cultural centers and permanent showrooms. There are also various interesting examples of innovations in the design of exhibition spaces whose goal is simply promotion with no link to a specific commercial or cultural product.

In a world with an economic system that requires permanent renovation and continuous advertising ploys, the ever-growing importance of portable architecture comes as no surprise, as it is limited to surrounding and framing products that are sold or promoted at an accelerating pace.

Ohne das fruchtbare Versuchsfeld einer auf kurze Dauer angelegten Architektur wären in den vergangenen 50 Jahren viele Innovationen im Bereich der Architektur und Innenarchitektur niemals bekannt geworden — oder hätten wesentlich länger gebraucht, bis sie sich durchgesetzt hätten. Schon seit über einem Jahrhundert gibt es wichtige Architekten, die die Möglichkeiten des Spiels, Versuchs und Experiments nutzen, welche die Gestaltung von Ausstellungsräumlichkeiten für Schauen und Präsentationen bietet. Zu diesem Zweig der Architektur zählen wahre Meilensteine, so der finnische Pavillon von Alvar Aalto für die Biennale von Venedig oder der deutsche Pavillon für die Weltausstellung von Barcelona 1929, die beide nach wie vor bestehen. Wenn die größten schöpferischen Talente sich oft an dieser Art von Arbeiten beteiligen, dann deshalb, weil diese den Schritt zwischen dem Modellbau und der Konstruktion großer Gebäude verkörpern, und das verleiht ihrer Kreativität Flügel.

Zur Gestaltung von Ausstellungsräumen gehören andererseits besondere Herausforderungen; dazu zählen das beschränkte Budget, begrenzter Platz und die Notwendigkeit, dass die Bauten von sehr kleinen Arbeitsmannschaften rasch auf- und wieder abgebaut werden können. Dieser Umstand hat zur Konsequenz, dass dieser Zweig der Architektur als ein Spiel verstanden wird.

Der vorliegende Band präsentiert eine ausgewogene Zusammenstellung zeitgenössischer Beispiele aus dem kommerziellen Messebau und der Ausstellungsarchitektur im Kulturbereich. Die Unterschiede zwischen beiden sind evident: einerseits eine optimale Produktpräsentation mit dem Ziel des Verkaufs, andererseits eine bestmögliche Verbreitung von Ideen, Daten und Kunstwerken.

Diese spektakuläre Auswahl an Projekten beinhaltet sowohl kleinere Messestände, die versuchen, die Aufmerksamkeit des Besuchers auf einer großen Messe auf sich zu ziehen — wie zum Beispiel das Projekt Sci Fi —, als auch große Ausstellungsräume von fast musealen Ausmaßen — wie z.B. der BMW Pavillon. Die Mitte der Bandbreite decken temporäre Ausstellungen in Kulturzentren oder Dauerausstellungen zu Informationszwecken ab. Ebenfalls gezeigt wurden innovative Beispiele im Bereich der Ausstellungsarchitektur; dabei ging es darum, sie vorzustellen, ohne ein kommerzielles oder kulturelles Interesse für ein bestimmtes Produkt zu verfolgen.

Es verwundert nicht, dass in einer Welt, deren ökonomisches System zu dauernder Erneuerung und zu kontinuierlicher Werbung zwingt, eine Architektur, die nicht auf Dauer angelegt ist, immer wichtiger wird — eine Architektur also, die sich darauf beschränkt, für das, was verkauft oder verbreitet werden soll, in einem zunehmend schwindelerregenden Tempo einen Rahmen zu bieten.

En los últimos cincuenta años, muchas de las innovaciones que se han implantado en arquitectura y en diseño de interiores jamás habrían visto la luz —o al menos habrían tardado mucho más tiempo en implementarse— de no haber sido por el fecundo banco de pruebas de la arquitectura efímera. Hace más de un siglo que apenas hay en el mundo arquitectos importantes que no hayan aprovechado las posibilidades de juego, tentativa y experimentación que brinda el diseño de recintos de exposición para muestras y exhibiciones. De hecho, esta rama de la arquitectura cuenta con grandes hitos como el Pabellón de Finlandia de Alvar Aalto para la Bienal de Venecia y el Pabellón de Alemania de la Exposición Internacional de Barcelona de 1929. Tal es la importancia de estas dos muestras de arquitectura efímera que ambas siguen en pie. Si los más grandes creadores acuden a menudo a este tipo de trabajos es porque éstos suelen encarnar el paso intermedio entre la creación de maquetas y la construcción de grandes edificios, lo cual da alas a su creatividad.

Por otra parte, el diseño de espacios de exhibición presenta dificultades añadidas que se convierten en verdaderos retos para sus creadores, como las limitaciones en el presupuesto, la falta de espacio y la proverbial necesidad de que las estructuras se instalen de forma rápida y se puedan desmontar por un equipo reducido de trabajadores. Esta circunstancia redunda en la visión de esta rama de la arquitectura como un juego.

Este volumen muestra una equilibrada combinación de ejemplos re?cientes de muestras comerciales y de instalaciones culturales. Las diferencias entre ambas resultan evidentes, pues en el primer caso existe una voluntad de dotar los productos con la mejor presentación posible para que éstos se vendan, mientras que en el segundo se trabaja para crear la mejor transmisión posible de ideas, datos y obras de arte para que éstos se difundan.

La espectacular selección de proyectos del presente libro incluye tanto los pequeños *stands* que tratan de capturar la atención del visitante en una gran feria —por ejemplo, el proyecto Sci Fi— como el gran recinto de exhibición de proporciones museísticas —como el BMW Pavilion—, pasando por exposiciones temporales en centros culturales y muestras permanentes en centros de divulgación. También figuran varios ejemplos interesantes de innovaciones en el diseño de espacios de exposición que se exhibieron *per se*, para darse a conocer, sin acompañar ningún producto comercial o cultural.

En un mundo cuyo sistema económico obliga a la renovación permanente y al continuo reclamo publicitario, no extraña que cada vez sea más importante la arquitectura que *no dura*, la que se limita a envolver y enmarcar, a un ritmo cada vez más vertiginoso, lo que se vende y se difunde.

Parmi les innovations qui sont apparues dans les domaines de l'architecture et de la décoration ces cinquante dernières années, beaucoup n'auraient jamais vu le jour (ou auraient mis beaucoup plus de temps à le faire) si elles n'étaient pas passées par le banc d'essai de l'architecture éphémère. Depuis plus d'un siècle, rares sont les architectes importants qui n'ont pas profité des possibilités de jeu et d'expérimentation qu'offrent les espaces d'exposition. Cette branche de l'architecture compte d'ailleurs des projets qui ont fait date, comme le Pavillon de la Finlande d'Alvar Aalto pour la Biennale de Venise, ou le Pavillon de l'Allemagne pour l'Exposition universelle de Barcelone de 1929. Ces deux exemples d'architecture éphémère ont du reste revêtu une telle importance qu'ils existent toujours aujourd'hui. Si les plus grands créateurs s'attèlent fréquemment à ce type de projets, c'est parce qu'ils sont souvent une étape intermédiaire entre la construction de maquettes et l'édification de grands bâtiments et, en cela, ils donnent des ailes à leur créativité.

D'autre part, les espaces d'exposition comportent leurs propres difficultés, qui supposent de véritables défis pour leurs créateurs, notamment les limites budgétaires, le manque d'espace et, bien sûr, le besoin de structures qui puissent s'installer et se démonter facilement, rapidement, et avec un minimum de main-d'œuvre. Ce sont ces difficultés qui assimilent cette branche de l'architecture à un jeu.

Cet ouvrage présente une combinaison équilibrée d'exemples très récents d'expositions commerciales et d'installations culturelles. Les différences entre les unes et les autres s'imposent d'elles-mêmes, car les premières ont pour objectif de présenter des produits sous la meilleure lumière possible (pour les vendre), et les secondes travaillent sur la transmission des idées, des informations et des œuvres d'art (pour les diffuser).

La sélection spectaculaire de projets que le lecteur trouvera dans ce livre explore un vaste éventail de formats, des petits *stands* qui tentent d'attirer l'attention des visiteurs dans un grand salon (comme le projet de Sci Fi), jusqu'aux espaces d'exposition aux dimensions gigantesques (comme le BMW Pavilion), en passant par des expositions temporaires dans des centres culturels et des expositions permanentes dans des centres scientifiques. Il y trouvera également plusieurs exemples intéressants d'innovations dans la conception d'espaces d'exposition qui ont été présentés pour eux-mêmes, sans accompagner aucun produit commercial ou culturel.

Dans un monde où le système économique oblige à une rénovation permanente et à une publicité continue, il n'est pas étonnant que l'architecture qui *ne dure pas* prenne une importance sans cesse croissante. Elle enveloppe et encadre les produits qui se vendent et se diffusent à un rythme de plus en plus vertigineux.

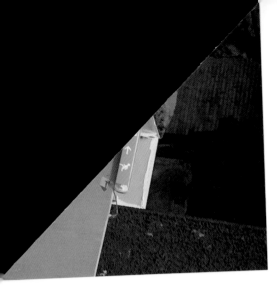

Nell'arco degli ultimi cinquant'anni, numerose innovazioni nel campo dell'Architettura e del design d'interni non ci sarebbero mai state (o almeno avrebbero richiesto tempi molto più lunghi) se non fosse stato per il fecondo banco di prova dell'Architettura effimera. Da oltre un secolo, è esiguo il numero di architetti di spicco che, su scala mondiale, non abbia messo a frutto i giochi, i tentativi e gli esperimenti offerti dalla progettazione di spazi espositivi per mostre ed esibizioni. Di fatto, tale ramo dell'Architettura vanta pietre miliari quali il Padiglione della Finlandia, costruito da Alvar Aalto per la Biennale di Venezia e il Padiglione della Germania, eretto in concomitanza con l'Esposizione Internazionale di Barcellona del 1929. Il rilievo di questi due esempi di Architettura effimera è tale che entrambi sono tuttora visibili. Spesso, i più insigni creatori si cimentano con questa tipologia di opere, che stanno a metà strada tra la creazione di plastici e la costruzione di strutture di grandi proporzioni e consentono ai loro artefici di dare libero sfogo alla loro creatività.

D'altro canto, la progettazione di spazi espositivi presenta ulteriori difficoltà, vere e proprie sfide per i loro creatori quali le restrizioni budgetarie, la mancanza di spazio e la necessità di far sì che tanto le operazioni di allestimento quanto quelle di smontaggio delle strutture possano essere espletate celermente e agevolmente da squadre composte da un numero alquanto ridotto di addetti. Tale fatto fa sì che questo ramo dell'Architettura sia percepito come un gioco.

Quest'opera ha lo scopo di offrire una combinazione equilibrata di esempi recentissimi, sia di natura commerciale sia di allestimenti culturali. Le differenze tra gli uni e gli altri sono evidenti, dal momento che i primi si adoperano per dotare alcuni prodotti della migliore veste possibile (affinché si vendano), mentre i secondi gravitano attorno alla migliore trasmissione possibile di idee, dati e opere d'arte (affinché si diffondano).

Nella mirabile selezione di progetti operata nell'ambito di questo testo, rientrano sia gli *stand* di piccole dimensioni, volti a richiamare l'attenzione del visitatore in un salone fieristico di grandi proporzioni (quale il progetto Sci Fi) sia il vasto spazio espositivo di proporzioni museali (quale il BMW Pavilion), oltre a mostre temporanee in centri culturali e mostre permanenti in centri di divulgazione. Vi si rinvengono anche vari esempi interessanti di innovazioni nella progettazione di spazi espositivi fini a se stessi, allestiti semplicemente per farsi conoscere, senza presentare nessun prodotto commerciale e culturale.

In un sistema economico che costringe a rinnovarsi costantemente e a un'incessante réclame pubblicitaria, non sorprende l'importanza crescente dell'Architettura *non durevole*, quella che si limita ad avvolgere e a incorniciare, a un ritmo sempre più vertiginoso, quanto si vende e si diffonde.

Atelier Brückner | Stuttgart
Bach House, Permanent exhibition
Eisenach, Germany | 2007

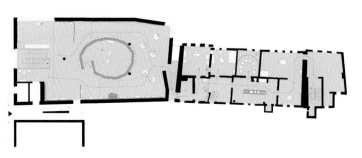

Established in 1907, the composer's house/museum has been expanded with a new building and a fabulous permanent exhibition. In line with the new configuration, the top floor of the pre-existing building houses a reconstruction of the historical context in which the musician's life unfolded, while the new building offers a look at his work, with a series of scores and instruments that flow from one to another like one of his famous fugues.

Das im Jahr 1907 gegründete Museum zum Leben und Werk Johann Sebastian Bachs wurde durch einen Anbau sowie eine komplett neue Dauerausstellung erweitert. Im oberen Stockwerk erhält der Besucher einen historischen Einblick in das Leben des Komponisten, während der Neubau einen Rundgang durch sein Werk vorsieht. Zahlreiche Partituren und Instrumente lassen ahnen, wie die berühmten Kompositionen Bachs entstanden sind.

Establecida en 1907, la casa-museo del compositor ha sido ampliada con un nuevo edificio y una flamante exposición permanente. Según la actual configuración, el piso superior del edificio existente alberga una reconstrucción del contexto histórico en que se desarrolló la vida del músico, mientras que el edificio nuevo ofrece un recorrido por su obra, con una serie de partituras e instrumentos que se suceden como una de sus famosas fugas.

La maison-musée du compositeur, créée en 1907, s'est vu adjoindre un nouveau corps de bâtiment et une nouvelle exposition permanente. L'étage supérieur de l'ancien bâtiment abrite une reconstitution du contexte historique dans lequel le musicien a vécu, et le nouveau bâtiment propose un parcours à travers son œuvre, avec une série de partitions et d'instruments qui se succèdent comme dans l'une de ses fameuses fugues.

Realizzata nel 1907, la casa-museo del compositore è stata ampliata con un nuovo edificio e una magnifica mostra permanente. In base alla configurazione attuale, il piano superiore dell'edificio preesistente ospita una ricostruzione del contesto storico in cui si svolse la vita del musicista, mentre il nuovo edificio offre un percorso attraverso la sua opera, con una serie di spartiti e strumenti che si susseguono come in una delle sue famose fughe.

Atelier Brückner | Stuttgart
Panasonic 2007, IFA (International Radio Exhibition)
Berlin, Germany | 2007

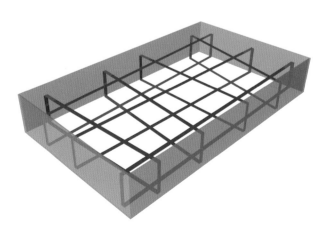

Under the slogan "Living in High Definition", Panasonic used IFA 2007 to present a large blue box in 16:9 proportion — an allusion to the panoramic format of the TV screens it markets. The floor, walls and grid that joined the different exhibition areas together were colored the company's trademark blue. A 50x16-foot screen covered nearly all the available space.

Unter dem Motto „Leben in Highresolution" präsentierte sich Panasonic auf der IFA 2007 mit einer großformatigen „Blue Box", deren Maßverhältnisse in Anspielung auf das Panoramaformat der Bildschirme, die von der Marke vertrieben werden, 16:9 betrugen. Der Boden, die Wände und das Raster, das die verschiedenen Oberflächen der Ausstellung verbindet, waren in dem charakteristischen Blauton der Firma gehalten. Ein fast 15 Meter langer und 5 Meter hoher Bildschirm nahm fast den gesamten verfügbaren Raum ein.

Bajo el lema «vivir en alta definición», Panasonic se presetó en el IFA de 2007 con una caja azul de grandes dimensiones, en proporción 16:9 (en alusión al formtato panorámico de las pantallas que comercializa la marca). Tanto el suelo como las paredes y la cuadrícula que une las distintas superficies de exposición son del azul característico de la firma. Una pantalla de casi 15 m de longitud y 5 m altura recorre casi todo el espacio disponible.

La présence de Panasonic à l'IFA 2007 avait pour thème « la vie en haute définition », et a pris la forme d'une grande boîte de proportions 16 : 9 (en référence au format panoramique des écrans que la marque commercialise). Le sol, les murs et le quadrillage qui relie les différentes surfaces sont du même bleu caractéristique de la marque. Un écran de presque 15 mètres de long et 5 mètres de haut parcourt presque tout l'espace disponible.

Con il motto «Vivere in alta definizione», Panasonic si è presentata all'IFA 2007 con una scatola di colore blu dalle grande dimensioni, in proporzione 16:9 (un'allusione al formato panoramico degli schermi venduti da tale marca). Il colore blu corporativo che la contraddistingue caratterizza il pavimento, le pareti nonché il reticolato volto a unire le varie superfici espositive. Uno schermo lungo quasi 15 m e alto 5 m si snoda praticamente in tutto lo spazio.

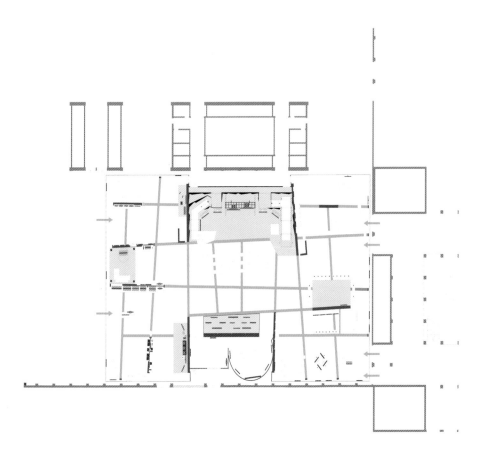

Watching TV with Family

Wide Viewing Angle

Atelier Brückner | Stuttgart
Dinosaurs, State Museum of Natural History
Stuttgart, Germany | 2007

33

The discovery of fossils in Baden-Württemberg was the basis for the central theme of this exhibition. Along a curved area, visitors explore the exhibition with increasing interest. Beginning with a collection from the Stuttgart State Museum of Natural History, the route passes a 'color door' that emits light and heat, symbolizing the warm era that motivated the development of the dinosaurs, and moves on in a strict chronological progression.

Die Entdeckungen von Fossilien in Baden-Württemberg sind das Hauptthema dieser Ausstellung. Der Raum ist als Kurve angelegt. Der Besucher durchläuft die streng chronologisch angeordnete Schau mit zunehmendem Interesse. Mit der Sammlung des Staatlichen Naturkundemuseums von Stuttgart als Ausgangspunkt durchschreitet man ein „Tor der Wärme", das Licht und Wärme ausstrahlt und die warme Ära symbolisiert, in der sich die Entwicklung der Dinosaurier vollzog.

Los descubrimientos de fósiles de Baden-Württemberg marcan el tema central de esta exhibición. A lo largo de una superficie curva, el visitante recorre la muestra cada vez con mayor interés. Partiendo de la colección del Museo Estatal de Historia Natural de Stuttgart, se pasa por una «puerta de calor» (emisora de luz y calefacción) que simboliza la era cálida que motivó el desarrollo de los dinosaurios, y se avanza siguiendo una rigurosa progresión cronológica.

Cette exposition a pour thème principal les fossiles découverts au Bade-Wurtemberg. Tout le long d'une surface incurvée les visiteurs explorent un parcours dont l'intérêt ne fait que croître. Après la collection du Musée national d'histoire naturelle de Stuttgart, on passe par une « porte de chaleur » (qui émet de la lumière et de la chaleur) qui symbolise l'ère chaude durant laquelle les dinosaures se sont développés, puis par une progression rigoureusement chronologique.

I fossili scoperti da Baden-Württemberg rappresentano l'argomento di fondo di questa esposizione. Lungo una superficie ricurva, l'interesse del visitatore nei confronti di questa mostra si fa sempre più vivo. Partendo dalla collezione del Museo statale di storia naturale di Stuttgart, si attraversa una «porta di calore» (che emette luce e calore) e simboleggia l'era temperata che favorì lo sviluppo dei dinosauri per poi ripercorrere, in rigorosa progressione cronologica.

Riffe

Im Gebiet der heutigen Schwäbischen Alb hatte sich während der Zeit des Weißen Juras am Meeresboden ein bewegtes Relief aus Schwammriff-Hügeln gebildet. Als das Gebiet sich hob, gerieten manche dieser Riffe in die Nähe des Meeresspiegels. Jetzt konnten sich die wegen ihrer Symbiose mit Algen von Sonnenlicht abhängigen Riffkorallen ansiedeln. Manche Hügel tauchten sogar als Inseln auf. Andernorts bildeten sich tiefe, vom offenen Wasser fast abgeschlossene Lagunen. Diese Differenzierung der Lebensräume in Korallenriffe, Schwammriffe und Lagunen führte zu einem großen Artenreichtum.

Korallen

Abhängig von Wassertiefe, Brandung und Durchlichtung entstanden im tropischen Weißjura-Meer zahlreiche kleine, isolierte Fleckenriffe, deren Durchmesser in der Regel zehn Meter nicht überschritt. In den Riffen und den von ihnen ausgehenden Schuttfächern bildeten sich verschiedenste kleinräumige ökologische Nischen. Im Stillwasser siedelten eher dünnästige und fächerförmige Korallen, an stärkerer Strömung ausgesetzten Stellen dagegen robuste Einzelkorallen oder massige oder dickästige Kolonien.

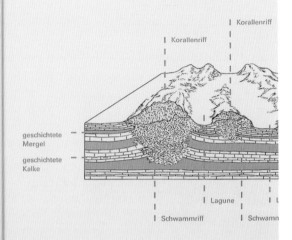

Korallenriff Korallenriff Korallenriff

geschichtete Mergel

geschichtete Kalke

Lagune L

Schwammriff Schwamm

Korallenkolonie
Thecosmilia trichotoma
Oberer Weißer Jura
Gerstetten, Landkreis Heidenheim,
östliche Schwäbische Alb

Bei kolonialen Formen sind mehrere
Polypen am Aufbau des Skelettes
beteiligt. Zwischen den dicken Ästen
von Thecosmilia siedelte häufig die
mit stabilen Byssusfäden angeheftete
Miesmuschel Arcomytilus furcatus.

Einzelkoralle
Montlivaltia spec.
Oberer Weißer Jura
Ettlenschieß und Dornstadt,
Alb-Donau-Kreis, Schwäbische Alb

Bei Einzelkorallen wie Montlivaltia
ist nur ein einziges Korallentier, ein
Polyp, an der Bildung des kalkigen
Skeletts beteiligt. Die Wuchsformen
sind sehr variabel.

Korallenkolonie
Enallhelia elegans
Oberer Weißer Jura
Gerstetten, Landkreis Heidenheim,
östliche Schwäbische Alb

Alle Arten der Gattung Enallhelia
zeigen zwei völlig unterschiedliche
Wuchsformen: im Stillwasser grazile aufrechte Fächer, im bewegten
Wasser knauelige Kolonien.

Korallenkolonie
Isastrea helianthoides
Oberer Weißer Jura
Gerstetten, Landkreis Heidenheim,
östliche Schwäbische Alb

Wie viele an bewegtes Wasser
angepasste Korallenkolonien bildet
auch Isastrea knollig-massige
Kalkskelette.

This is the first museum in China dedicated wholly to the automobile. A timeline marks the route of the permanent exhibition. Each piece on display forms part of a particular spatial framework conceived to emphasize it so that the different cars create vignettes of real visual impact. The exhibition is arranged to give visitors the feeling of travelling through time as they move from one room to another.

Als erstes Museum in China widmet sich das Shanghai Auto Museum dem Automobil. Ein Zeitstrahl zieht sich durch den gesamten Ausstellungsbereich. Für jedes Exponat wurde eine individuelle, räumlich begrenzte Ausstellungsumgebung geschaffen, sodass die charakteristischen Eigenheiten der einzelnen Autos optisch besonders gut zu Geltung kommen. Die Anordnung der Ausstellung vermittelt dem Besucher während seines Rundgangs den Eindruck, eine Reise durch die Zeit zu erleben.

Éste es el primer museo de China dedicado íntegramente al automóvil. Una línea temporal marca el recorrido de la muestra permanente. Cada pieza expuesta se inserta en un determinado marco espacial concebido para realzarla, de forma que los distintos coches crean estampas con un verdadero impacto visual. Por medio de la disposición del conjunto se logra que el visitante experimente la sensación de viajar a través del tiempo al transitar por las salas.

Ceci est le premier musée chinois consacré exclusivement à l'automobile. Une ligne temporelle trace le parcours de l'exposition permanente. Chaque pièce exposée s'insère dans un cadre spatial conçu pour la mettre en valeur, de sorte que les voitures créent des tableaux visuellement très efficaces. La disposition d'ensemble donne aux visiteurs l'impression de voyager dans le temps en passant par les différentes salles.

Questo è il primo museo della Cina dedicato completamente all'automobile. Il percorso della mostra permanente è stato concepito in funzione di una linea cronologica. Ogni pezzo esposto è inserito in una determinata cornice spaziale, appositamente pensata per dargli risalto, in modo tale che le varie auto creano delle stampe caratterizzate da un forte impatto visivo. Mediante la disposizione dell'insieme, il visitante può provare la sensazione di viaggiare nel tempo passando da una sala all'altra.

序—人类移动方式的变革
PROLOGUE - THE EVOLUTION OF HUMAN TRANSPORT SYSTEMS

RIVING

银石赛道
SILVERSTONE

年代 YEAR	时间 TIME
1950	2:13'23.600
1955	3:07'21.200
1960	2:04'24.300
1965	2:05'25.400
1970	1:57'02.000
1975	1:22'05.000
1980	1:34'49.228
1985	1:18'10.436
1990	1:18'30.999
1995	1:35'35.093
2000	1:28'50.108
2005	1:24'29.588

FINA
FINA
MICHELIN
WARSTEINER

Bonjoch Associats | Barcelona
Elisava Stand, Estudia Teaching Trade Fair
Barcelona, Spain | 2007

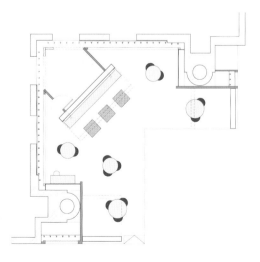

An L-shaped space located in a corner of the trade-fair pavilion was the setting chosen for this stand covering barely 600 square feet. The installation was designed to attract a young public to the different university orientation programs and teaching offers. The design was based on three red rings on a backlit area. The silhouettes of visitors and staff appear against the background.

Als Rahmen wählte man eine L-Form für den knapp 55 Quadratmeter großen Stand, der in einer Ecke des Messepavillons liegt. Mit der Installation versuchte man, die Aufmerksamkeit eines jungen Publikums auf verschiedene Programme der universitären Ausrichtung und auf Lehrangebote zu richten. Das Design basiert auf drei roten Bögen im Gegenlicht. Die Silhouetten der Besucher und des Service-Personals wirken vor diesem Hintergrund scherenschnittartig.

Un espacio en forma de L ubicado en una esquina del pabellón ferial fue el marco escogido para este stand de apenas 55 m² de superficie. Con la instalación se pretendió llamar la atención de un público joven hacia los distintos programas de orientación universitaria y las ofertas docentes. El diseño se basa en tres arcos rojos sobre un contraluz. Las siluetas de los visitantes y del personal de atención aparecen recortadas sobre el fondo.

Ce stand d'à peine 55 m² de surface est logé dans un espace en forme de L dans un coin du pavillon d'exposition. L'installation avait pour objectif d'attirer l'attention d'un public jeune sur les différents programmes d'orientation universitaire et sur les offres d'enseignement. Le concept se compose de trois arcs rouges, et les silhouettes des visiteurs et du personnel d'accueil se découpent en contre-jour sur le fond.

Con questo stand di soli 55 m² di superficie, allestito in uno spazio a «L» ubicato in uno degli angoli del padiglione fieristico, s'intendeva richiamare l'interesse di un pubblico giovane verso i vari programmi d'orientamento universitario e le offerte pedagogiche. Il progetto si basa su tre archi di colore rosso su controluce. Le sagome dei visitatori e dello staff di servizio si stagliano sul fondo.

ELISAVA
Escola Superior de Disseny

Centre adscrit a la

UNIVERSITAT
POMPEU FABRA

Graduat Superior en Disseny

Enginyeria Tècnica en
Disseny Industrial

Arquitectura Tècnica

Màsters i Postgraus

Cicles Formatius en Disseny

↘
www.elisava.net

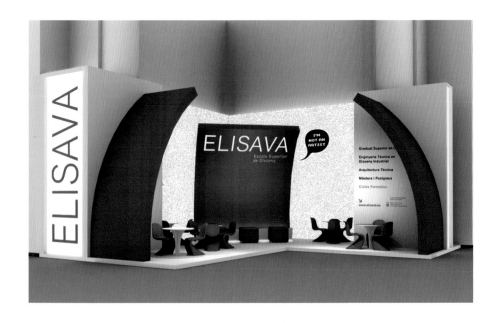

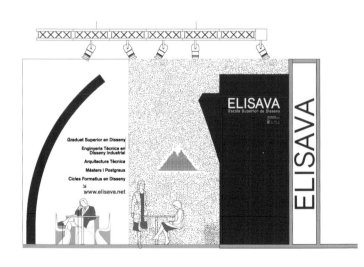
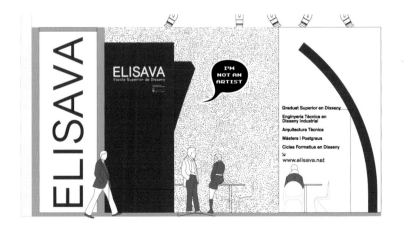

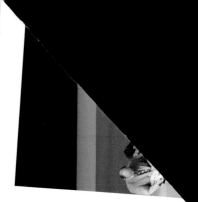

Bo
Indentity De/Coding, International Furniture
Copenhagen, Denmark | 2005

Bosch & Fjord's intention behind this exhibition was to create a linear route around the different exhibition spaces of the event it forms part of. The main path through the exhibition changes from yellow to blue and orange to brown and pink, colors that symbolize the five different visitor identities according to the creators, i.e., "directors", "hippies", "business-women", "dreamers" and "yuppies".

Diese Ausstellung fügt sich eine größere Veranstaltung ein. Die Absicht von Bosch & Fjord bestand darin, einen linearen Weg durch die verschiedenen Räume anzulegen. Der Leitfaden durch die Ausstellung verläuft von Gelb zu Blau, Orange, Braun und Rosa. Diese Farben symbolisieren die verschiedenen Identitäten der Besucher (den Gestaltern zufolge „der Direktor", „der Hippie", „die Geschäftsfrau", „der Idealist" und „der Yuppie").

La intención de Bosch & Fjord con esta muestra fue la de crear un recorrido lineal a través de los distintos espacios de exhibición del evento en el que se inserta. El hilo conductor de la exhibición cambia del amarillo al azul, y luego al naranja, marrón y al rosa, colores que simbolizan las cinco identidades diferentes de los visitantes (según los creadores, «el director», «el hippie», «la mujer de negocios», «el idealista» y «el yuppie»).

Pour cette exposition, l'intention de Bosch & Fjord était de créer un parcours linéaire à travers les différents espaces de l'événement qui lui sert de cadre. Le fil conducteur de l'exposition passe du jaune au bleu, puis à l'orange, ou marron et au rose, des couleurs qui symbolisent les cinq identités des visiteurs (selon les créateurs, « le directeur », « le hippie », « la femme d'affaires », « l'idéaliste » ou « le yuppie »).

Con questa esposizione, la Bosch & Fjord era intenzionata a tracciare un percorso lineare nei vari spazi espositivi della manifestazione in cui s'inserisce. Il filo conduttore della mostra cambia dal giallo al blu, all'arancione, a le marrone e al rosa, colori che simbolizzano le cinque identità diverse dei visitatori (secondo i creatori, «il manager», «l'hippy», «la donna d'affari», «l'idealista» e «lo yuppie»).

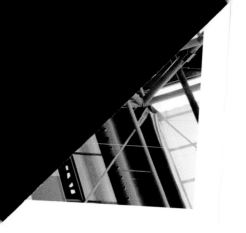

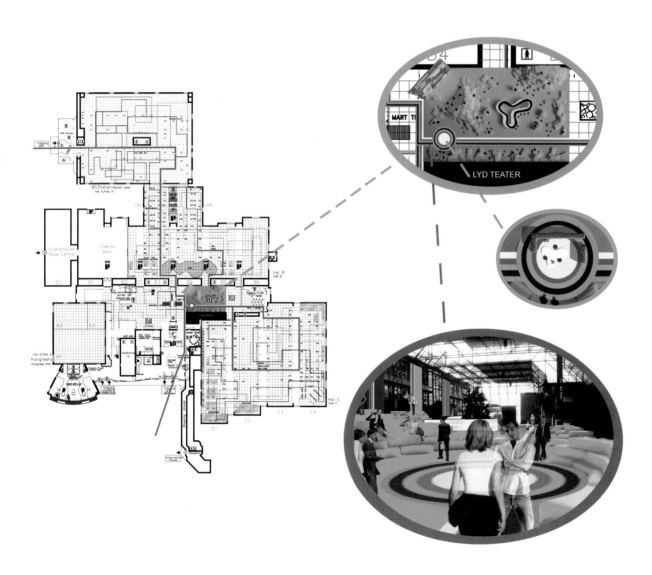

MART T

LYD TEATER

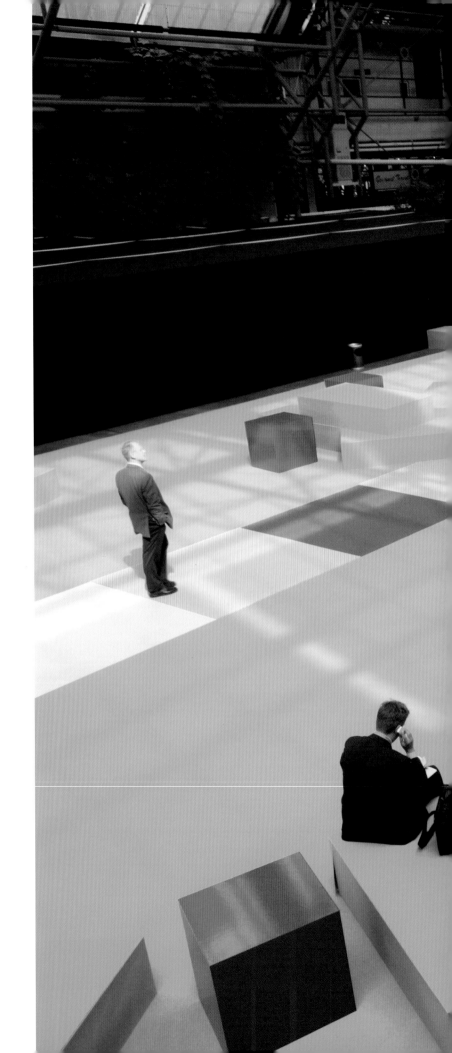

Bosch & Fjord | Copenhagen
Use It!, Expo 2005
Tokyo, Japan | 2005

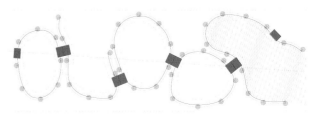

The structure of this exhibition space consists of flexible fiberglass walls. Divided into five areas, they each encourage visitors to touch the objects on display, a series of examples of Danish design, thus involving the public directly. The five areas are: movement produces development, reflection produces understanding, limitation produces innovation, help produces independence and dialogue produces inspiration.

Die Grundstruktur der Ausstellungsarchitektur bilden Wände aus flexiblen Glasfasern. Die Ausstellung ist in fünf Bereiche untergliedert. In jedem wird der Besucher animiert, die Objekte – kleine Qualitätsproben von dänischem Design – zu berühren, um zu erreichen, dass er in das Ausstellungsthema einbezogen wird. Die fünf Räume befassen sich mit den Themen: Bewegung bewirkt Entwicklung, Reflexion bewirkt Verständnis, Beschränkung bewirkt Innovation, Hilfe bewirkt Unabhängigkeit und Dialog bewirkt Inspiration.

La estructura de este espacio de exhibición está compuesta por paredes de fibra de vidrio flexibles. Está dividida en cinco áreas, y en cada una se anima al visitante a tocar los objetos, pequeñas muestras de las cualidades del diseño danés, haciendo así que el visitante se involucre. Los cinco espacios son: el movimiento produce desarrollo, la reflexión produce comprensión, la limitación produce innovación, la ayuda produce independencia y el diálogo produce inspiración.

La structure de cet espace d'exposition se compose de murs flexibles en fibre de verre. Elle se divise en cinq parties qui invitent les visiteurs à toucher les objets, de petits échantillons de la qualité du design danois qui les encouragent à participer à l'exposition. Les 5 espaces sont : le mouvement produit le développement, la réflexion produit la compréhension, la limitation produit l'innovation, l'aide produit l'indépendance et le dialogue produit l'inspiration.

La struttura di questo spazio espositivo è fatta di pareti flessibili in fibra di vetro. Nelle cinque zone in cui si articola, il visitatore viene esortato a toccare gli oggetti, esempi a dimensioni ridotte delle qualità del design danese, e vi partecipa. I cinque spazi sono: il movimento produce sviluppo, la riflessione produce comprensione, la limitazione produce innovazione, l'aiuto produce indipendenza e il dialogo produce ispirazione.

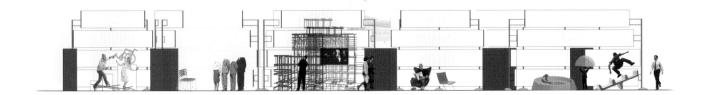

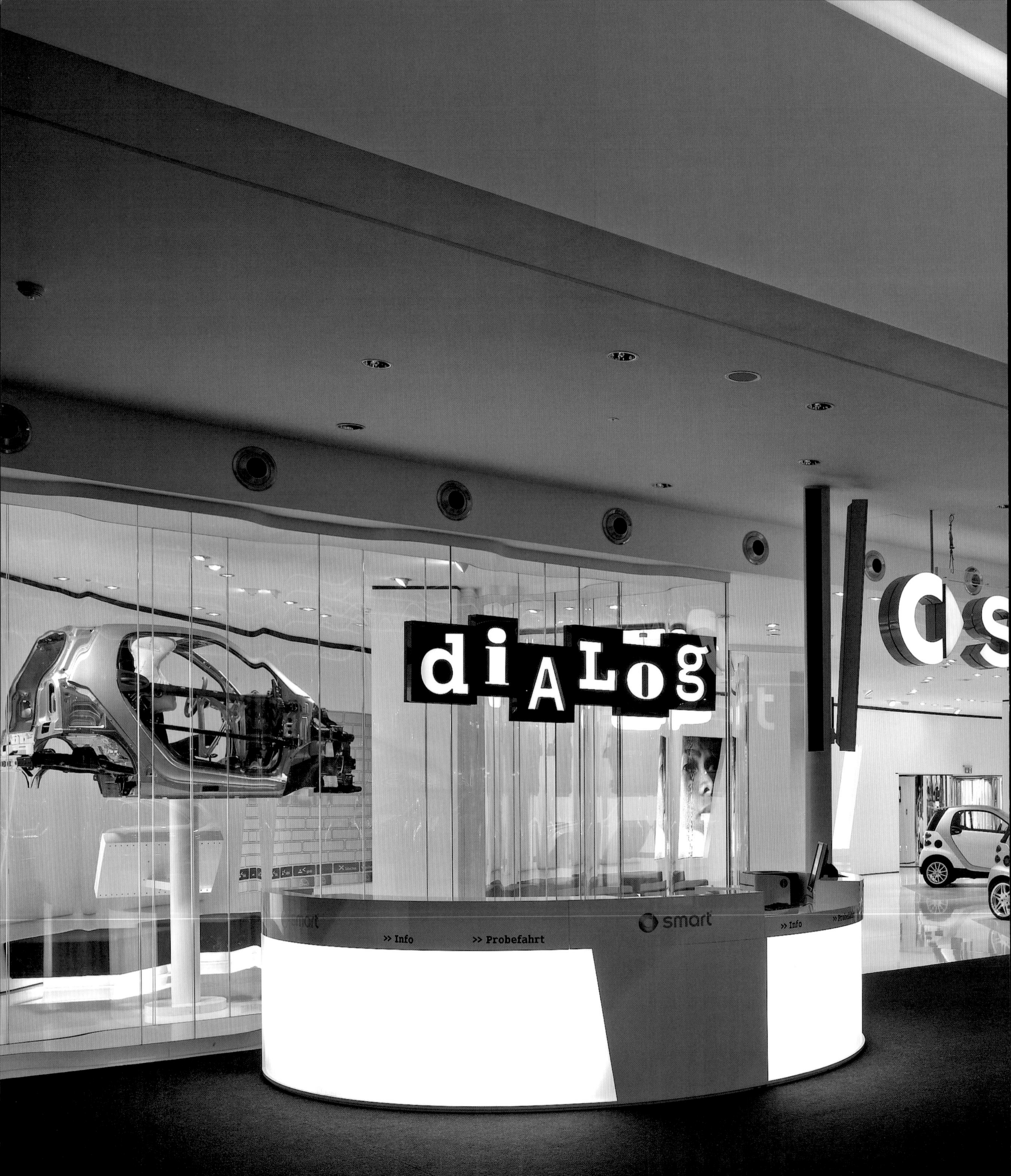
diALog
smart
>> Info
>> Probefahrt
>> Info

Braun & Wagner Designer-Partnerschaft | Aachen
Smart, International Motor Show
Frankfurt, Germany | 2007

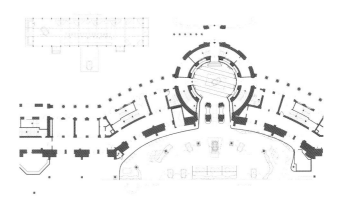

The main draw of the 2007 Frankfurt car show was the small vehicle installation of large car group Mercedes Benz. The architectural concept recalls the configuration of a store window. The undulating glass facades create division-free spaces, shaping a type of giant boutique where the goods on display are the carmaker's different models.

Hauptanziehungspunkt der Automobilmesse in Frankfurt 2007 war die Installation für den Kleinwagen der großen Mercedes-Gruppe. Das architektonische Konzept ließ an die Gestaltung eines Schaufensters denken. Die geschwungenen Glasfassaden bilden Räume, ohne sie abzuteilen, und verleihen dem Ganzen die Gestalt einer riesigen Boutique, in der die verschiedenen Auto-Modelle dieser Produktpalette die Exponate sind.

El principal reclamo de la feria automovilística de Frankfurt en 2007 fue la instalación del pequeño vehículo del gran grupo Mercedes. El concepto arquitectónico evoca la configuración de un escaparate. Las fachadas de cristal ondulante crean espacios sin compartimentarlos y dan forma a una especie de *boutique* gigante en la que los artículos expuestos son los distintos modelos de automóviles de la gama.

En 2007, la principale publicité du salon de l'automobile de Francfort était l'installation du petit véhicule du grand groupe Mercedes. Le concept architectural évoque une vitrine. Les façades en verre ondulantes créent des espaces sans pour autant compartimenter, et forment une sorte de boutique géante où les articles exposés sont les différents modèles de voiture de la gamme.

Il piccolo veicolo del grande gruppo Mercedes è stato la maggior attrazione del salone automobilistico di Francoforte del 2007. Il concetto architettonico rievoca la configurazione di una vetrina le cui facciate di vetro ondulante creano spazi senza dividerli in compartimenti, il che dà vita a una specie di *boutique* gigante in cui gli articoli esposti sono rappresentati dai vari modelli di automobili della gamma.

UnABHäNGiGkeIT

Célia Gomes | Lisbon
Expo Cidade/Expo Promotores, Architecture Triennale
Lisbon, Portugal | 2007

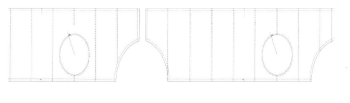

The main strategy in the design of these two joint exhibitions consisted in hiding their content as much as possible. The architects' initial intention was to avoid a previously determined route, to which end they created a type of labyrinth in which visitors can lose themselves. The two exhibitions coexist with no dividing elements, flowing together to generate the feeling of a single cultural proposal.

Die Hauptstrategie bei der Gestaltung der beiden Parallelausstellungen bestand darin, ihren Inhalt so weit wie möglich zu verstecken. Ein vorab markierter Rundweg sollte vermieden werden; so wurde eine Art Labyrinth geschaffen, in dem sich der Besucher (auch mental) verlieren kann. Die beiden Präsentationen sind nicht voneinander getrennt – der Grundgedanke war, dass sie beim Betrachter den Eindruck hervorrufen sollten, sich vor einem einzigen Kulturangebot zu befinden.

La principal estrategia en el diseño de estas dos exposiciones conjuntas consistía en ocultar al máximo su contenido. La intención de los arquitectos fue, desde el principio, evitar que hubiera un recorrido previamente marcado; así, crearon una especie de laberinto en el que el visitante pudiera abstraerse. Las dos exposiciones coexisten sin elementos divisorios, ya que la idea era que confluyeran para generar en el espectador la sensación de que está ante una sola propuesta cultural.

Pour ces deux expositions conjointes, la stratégie principale consistait à cacher le plus possible leur contenu. Dès le départ, l'intention des architectes était d'éviter tout parcours préétabli. Ils ont donc créé un labyrinthe où les visiteurs pourraient se perdre. Les deux expositions coexistent sans éléments de séparation, car l'idée était de les faire confluer, en donnant au spectateur l'impression de se trouver devant une seule et même proposition culturelle.

La strategia principale nella progettazione di queste due mostre connesse consisteva nell'occultarne al massimo il contenuto. Gli architetti erano intenzionati a evitare un percorso prestabilito, così hanno messo a punto un labirinto in cui il visitatore può isolarsi. Entrambe le mostre coesistono senza elementi divisori, dal momento che l'idea era la loro confluenza per generare nello spettatore la sensazione di trovarsi davanti a un'unica proposta culturale.

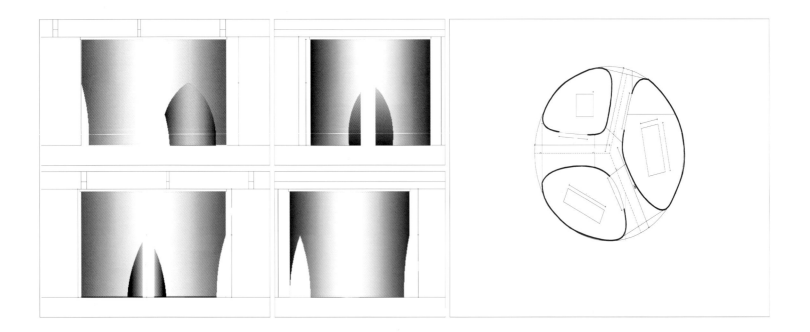

Chris Bosse, Students from UTS | Sydney
Origami, No event
Sydney, Australia | 2007

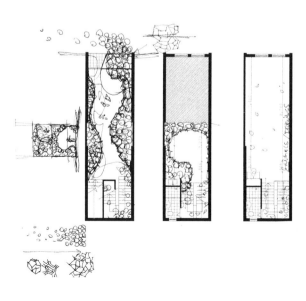

Under the guidance of professor Chris Bosse, design students from the University of Technology, Sydney used recycled cardboard to form a total of 3,500 molecules in two different shapes. The result was a series of rooms filled with geometric paper figures piled together and plastered on walls and ceilings, illuminated by neon lights.

Unter Anleitung von Chris Bosse, Professor an der Technischen Hochschule von Sydney, verwendeten seine Design-Studenten für diese Installation Recycling-Karton, um daraus insgesamt 3500 Moleküle in zwei unterschiedlichen Ausformungen zu konzipieren. Das Ergebnis bestand aus Räumen voller geometrischer Papierfiguren, die übereinander gestapelt wurden und an Wänden und Decken eingegipst waren. Sie wurden von Neonlampen beleuchtet.

Bajo la orientación del profesor Chris Bosse, los estudiantes de diseño de la Universidad de Tecnología de Sydney utilizaron para esta instalación cartón reciclado para formar un total de 3.500 moléculas de dos formas diferentes. El resultado consistió en habitaciones llenas de figuras geométricas de papel, apiladas unas sobre otras y enyesadas en paredes y techos iluminadas por luces de neón.

Sous la houlette de leur professeur Chris Bosse, les étudiants en design de l'Université de Technologie de Sydney ont créé pour cette installation 3 500 molécules en carton recyclé selon deux modèles différents. Le résultat : des pièces remplies de figures géométriques en papier, empilées les unes sur les autres et plâtrées sur les murs et aux plafonds, éclairées au néon.

Sotto la direzione del Professor Chris Bosse, in questo allestimento, gli studenti di design della University of Technology di Sydney, hanno impiegato cartone riciclato per creare complessivamente 3.500 molecole aventi due forme diverse. Ne sono derivate stanze colme di figure geometriche di carta, disposte le une sopra le altre, fissate con gesso su pareti e soffitti e illuminate da luci al neon.

Chris Bosse | Sydney
Paradise Pavilion, Entry 06 Exhibition
Zeche Zollverein, Germany | 2006

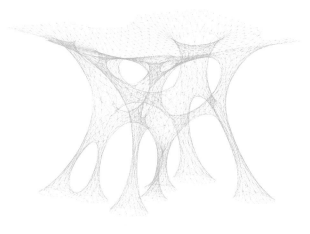

Structures formed of microscopic cells were the inspiration for the design of this pavilion, which brings to mind the irregular shapes found in sponges, coral and foam. The pavilion was designed by architect Chris Bosse who conceived these *biomorphic* shapes with the help of software systems that simulated shapes found in nature to generate architectural structures. The completed pavilion weighs only 37 lbs.

Inspirationsquelle für die Gestaltung dieses Pavillons waren mikroskopische Zellstrukturen; es werden die unregelmäßigen Formen von Schwämmen, Korallen oder Schaum evoziert. Der Entwurf des Pavillons stammt von dem Architekten Chris Bosse, der diese *biomorphen* Gebilde konzipierte, indem er unterschiedliche Software-Systeme gebrauchte, wobei er die Formen der Natur simulierte, um architektonische Strukturen zu generieren. Der gesamte Pavillon wiegt nur 17 Kilogramm.

Las estructuras formadas por células microscópicas sirvieron de inspiración para el diseño de este pabellón, que evoca formas irregulares como las de las esponjas, los corales y la espuma. El pabellón fue diseñado por el arquitecto Chris Bosse, que concibió estas formas *biomórficas* mediante la utilización de diversos sistemas de *software*, simulando las formas de la naturaleza para generar estructuras arquitectónicas. El pabellón al completo pesa solamente 17 kg.

Ce pavillon est inspiré des structures formées par les cellules microscopiques. Il évoque les formes irrégulières des éponges, des coraux ou de la mousse. Il a été conçu par l'architecte Chris Bosse. Ce dernier a créé ces formes *biomorphiques* grâce à plusieurs programmes qui simulent les formes de la nature pour générer des structures architecturales. Le pavillon ne pèse que 17 kilos en tout et pour tout.

Per il progetto di questo padiglione, rievocante forme irregolari come quelle delle spugne, dei coralli e della schiuma, l'architetto Chris Bosse si è ispirato alle strutture formate da cellule microscopiche e ha concepito queste forme *biomorfe* avvalendosi di vari sistemi di *software* e simulando le forme della natura per generare strutture architettoniche. Nel complesso, il padiglione pesa soltanto 17 kg.

Cut/Paste
CRYSTALLIZED™ Cosmos
TRENDS SPRING/SUMMER 2007

Cultural Sushi | Paris
Crystallized Cosmos, Asia's Fashion Jewellery & Accessories Fair
Hong Kong, China | 2005

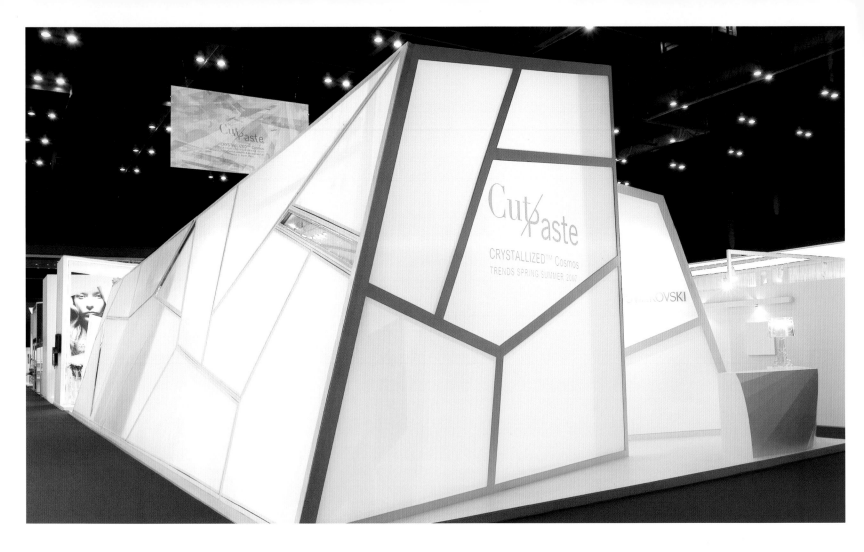

In its second year, the structural concept of this exhibition was based on asymmetry, reconstruction and the loss of direction of objects. The outside walls reflect the language Swarovski uses in its cut-glass works. Each wall features metal frames across which translucent fabric is stretched. The curved walls act as a screen for the projection of two informational videos.

Das Konzept dieser Ausstellungsarchitektur basiert auf Asymmetrie, Rekonstruktion und Verzicht auf eine bestimmte Ausrichtung der Objekte. Die Außenwände spiegeln die Sprache, die Swarovski bei seinen Werken aus geschnittenem Glas einsetzt. Jede Wand hat Metallrahmen, über die ein lichtdurchlässiger Stoff gespannt ist. Die gebogenen Wände dienen als Projektionsfläche für Infovideos.

En su segunda edición, el concepto de la estructura de esta exhibición se basa en la asimetría, reconstrucción y pérdida de dirección de los objetos. Las paredes exteriores reflejan el lenguaje utilizado por Swarovski en sus obras de cristal cortado. Cada pared posee unos marcos de metal sobre los que se tensa una tela translúcida. Las paredes curvas sirven de pantalla para la proyección de dos vídeos informativos.

Pour sa deuxième édition, le concept de la structure de cette exposition se base sur l'asymétrie, la reconstruction et la perte de direction des objets. Les murs extérieurs reflètent le langage que Swarovski utilisait dans ses créations en cristal taillé. Chacun d'entre eux est décoré de cadres de métal sur lesquels est tendue une toile translucide. Les murs incurvés servent d'écran de projection pour deux vidéos d'information.

Nella sua seconda edizione, il concetto strutturale di questa mostra poggia sull'asimmetria, sulla ricostruzione e sulla perdita d'orientamento degli oggetti. Le pareti esterne rispecchiano il linguaggio di cui si è servito Swarovski nelle sue opere di vetro tagliato. Ogni parete è dotata di cornici metalliche su cui viene tesa una tela traslucida. Dal canto loro, le pareti ricurve fungono da schermo per proiettarvi due filmati informativi.

Cut/Paste

CRYSTALLIZED™ Cosmos

TRENDS SPRING/SUMMER 2007

AN INITIATIVE BY SWAROVSKI

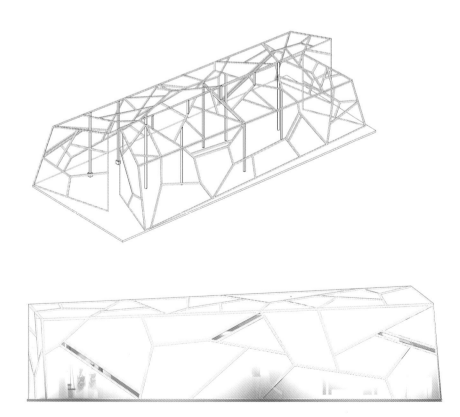

Curiosity | Tokyo
Nissan Booth, Tokyo Motor Show
Tokyo, Japan | 2007

With this exhibition space the architects set goals similar to the ones of the carmaker from whom they received the commission, i.e., to offer a design that could be used as an expression of Japanese culture and a meeting point between tradition and modernity. A large suspended ring framed the focal point of the site and concealed inside it a futuristic atmosphere. Models already under production were shown outside the ring perimeter.

Die Architekten verfolgten bei diesem Ausstellungsraum Ziele, vergleichbar mit jenen des Auftraggebers, eines Automobilunternehmens. Dafür entwickelten sie ein Design, das als Ausdrucksträger der japanischen Kultur fungiert und Verbindungsglied zwischen Tradition und Moderne ist. Ein großer schwebender, Ring umrahmt den Ausstellungsbereich und verwandelt den Raum in eine futuristische Atmosphäre. Bereits produzierte Modelle werden außerhalb dieser Zone vorgestellt.

Con este espacio de exposición los arquitectos se plantearon objetivos parecidos a los de la marca de automóviles que les encomendó el encargo: ofrecer un diseño que sirviera como expresión de la cultura jaonesa y de punto de unión entre tradición y modernidad. Un gran anillo suspendido marca el foco de atención del recinto, que presenta una atmósfera futurista. Los modelos ya en producción se muestran fuera del perímetro de este anillo.

Pour cet espace d'exposition les architectes se sont fixé des objectifs semblables à ceux de la marque automobile qui leur avait commandé le projet, notamment de proposer un concept qui reflète la culture japonaise et qui fait le lien entre tradition et modernité. Un grand anneau suspendu signale le centre de l'attention à l'atmosphère futuriste. Les modèles en production sont exposés en dehors du périmètre de cet anneau.

Con questo spazio espositivo gli architetti si erano prefissati obiettivi analoghi a quelli della marca di auto che aveva commissionato loro l'opera, come quello di esprimere la cultura giapponese e unire tradizione e modernità. Un anello sospeso di grandi proporzioni rappresenta il punto di richiamo di questo spazio che racchiude un'atmosfera futurista. I modelli già in produzione sono stati predisposti all'esterno del perimetro di questo anello.

121

Danish Architecture Centre | Copenhagen
MAD in China, Danish Architecture Centre
Copenhagen, Denmark | 2008

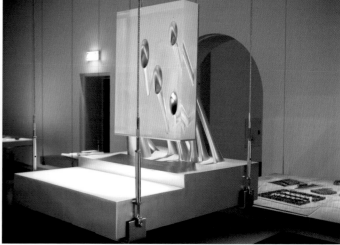

MAD Office is a firm of young architects and designers known for being the first studio of Chinese architects to win an international competition. The highlight here is the assembly of wooden bases suspended from the ceiling by metallic struts used to exhibit the models. This creates a contrast with the old wooden structures that fill the DAC space and causes a spectacular visual impact for whoever visits the installation.

MAD Office ist eine Firma junger Architekten und Designer, die als erstes chinesisches Büro einen internationalen Wettbewerb gewann. Die an metallenen Spannvorrichtungen von der Decke hängenden Modelle fallen auch dadurch ins Auge, dass sie an der Holzdeckenkonstruktion für dieses Ausstellungskonzept montiert wurden. Der Kontrast zu den alten Holzstrukturen des DAC hinterlässt bei jedem, der die Installation begeht, einen spektakulären visuellen Eindruck.

MAD Office es una firma de jóvenes arquitectos y diseñadores, conocidos por ser el primer despacho de arquitectos chinos en ganar un concurso internacional. De la exposición destaca el montaje, que consiste en unas bases de madera suspendidas del techo mediante tensores metálicos que muestran las maquetas. Esto establece un contraste con las antiguas estructuras de madera que llenan el espacio del DAC y produce un impacto visual espectacular a quien recorre la instalación.

MAD Office est un cabinet de jeunes architectes et designers. C'est le premier cabinet d'architecture chinois lauréat d'un concours international. L'exposition brille par son montage, avec des bases en bois pour montrer les maquettes suspendues au plafond par des tenseurs métalliques. Le contraste avec les vieilles structures en bois qui remplissent l'espace du DAC crée une image spectaculaire pour les visiteurs de l'installation.

I giovani architetti e progettisti della società MAD Office, sono famosi in quanto, per la prima volta, uno studio di architetti cinesi si è aggiudicato un concorso internazionale. A spiccare nell'esposizione è l'allestimento, in cui ci si è avvalsi di basi lignee per mostrare i plastici che pendono dal soffitto grazie a cavi metallici e creano un contrasto con le vecchie strutture in legno che colmano lo spazio DAC, con un impatto visivo spettacolare.

an'an men square: people's park

350M
450M
300M
500M
250M
200M
150M
100M
000M

200M

MAD IN CHINA

kinesiska visioner år 2050

3. november

Designrichtung GmbH | Zurich
D5 Exhibition, Designers' Saturday
Langenthal, Switzerland | 2006

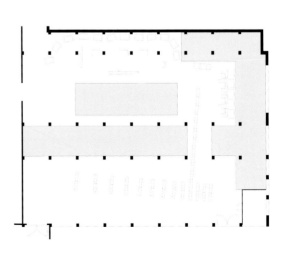

For this design exhibition, the firm Denz was granted a 6,400 square feet space in a warehouse. The architects divided it into three areas: exhibition, lounge and information zone. The first was used to present a single product: the new D5 storage system. To add a more human touch, it was filled with jam jars whose different colors helped underline the combination of white and red on which the whole of the exhibition was based.

Für diese Ausstellung gestand man der Firma Denz einen 600 Quadratmeter großen Raum in einem Warenlager zu. Die Architekten unterteilten das Geschoss in drei Zonen für Ausstellung, Lounge und Infobereich. Im ersten Bereich wird als einziges Produkt das neue Lagersystem D5 präsentiert. Um dieser Regalstruktur einen etwas menschlicheren Touch zu verleihen, füllte man sie mit Marmeladentöpfen, deren abwechselnde Farben dazu beitrugen, die Farbkombination aus Weiß und Rot zu unterstreichen, auf der die Ausstellung basiert.

Para esta muestra de diseñadores, a la firma Denz se le concedió el espacio de 600 m² de un almacén. Los arquitectos dividieron la planta en tres espacios: exhibición, *lounge* y punto informativo. En la primera zona se presenta un solo producto: el nuevo sistema de almacenaje D5. Para dar un toque más humano, se llenó de tarros de mermelada cuyos colores se alternan para subrayar así la combinación de blanco y rojo en la que se basa toda la muestra.

Pour cette exposition de designers, la marque Denz s'est vu attribuer un espace de 600 m² dans un entrepôt. Les architectes ont divisé la surface en trois espaces : exposition, lounge et zone d'information. Le premier espace présente le produit (seulement un) : le nouveau système de rangement D5. Il a été rempli de pots de confiture dont les couleurs alternées aident à souligner la combinaison de rouge et de blanc sur laquelle se base toute l'exposition.

Per quest'esposizione di designer, alla società Denz è stato assegnato uno spazio di 600 m² di un magazzino merci. Gli architetti hanno suddiviso la pianta in tre spazi (esibizione, *lounge* e zona informativa) di cui il primo accoglie il prodotto (uno solo): il nuovo sistema di stoccaggio D5. Per conferire un tocco più umano, le mensole sono state colmate di barattoli di marmellata a colori alterni che sottolineano l'abbinamento bianco-rosso su cui si basa l'intera mostra.

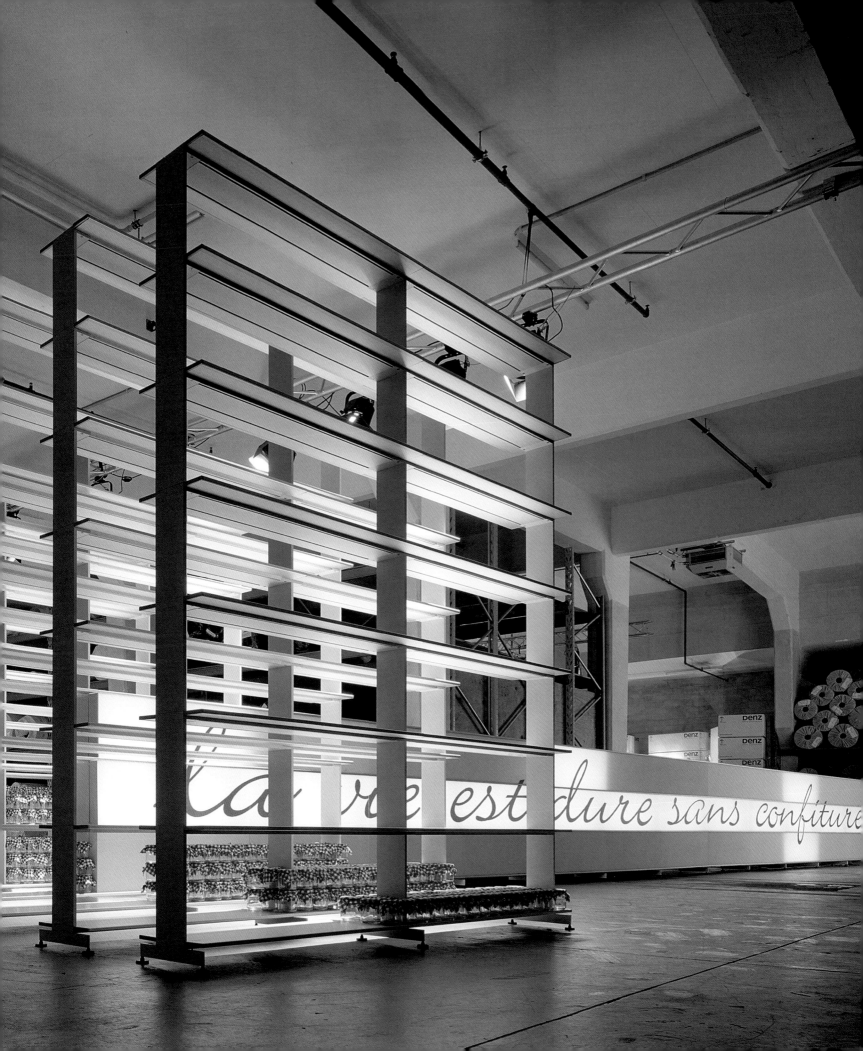

Designrichtung GmbH | Zurich
Denz Showroom, No event
Gümligen, Switzerland | 2005

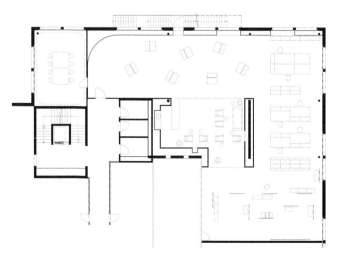

The designers of this project were commissioned to come up with a showroom that would offer a common meeting area for a sales force specializing in office furniture and a work space for the brand's furniture designers, as well as those from its lighting division Se'lux. The facilities feature an exhibition zone with a brightly sequined wall and a minimalist black cube in the center.

Der Auftrag, den die Designer dieses Projekts übernahmen, bestand darin, einen Showroom zu konzipieren, der einen Gemeinschaftsbereich bieten sollte. Dort kann sich das auf Büromöbeldesign spezialisierte Verkaufsteam treffen, außerdem wird ein Arbeitsraum für die Möbeldesigner der Firma und ihre Beleuchtungsabteilung Se'lux geboten. Die Einbauten umfassen einen Ausstellungsbereich, bei dem eine leuchtende Wand aus Pailletten und ein zentraler, minimalistisch anmutender schwarzer Kubus hervorstechen.

El encargo encomendado a los diseñadores de este proyecto consistió en concebir un *showroom* que ofreciera un área de reunión común para los comerciales especializados en muebles de oficina, así como un espacio de trabajo para los diseñadores de la marca y de Se'lux, su división de iluminación. Las instalaciones cuentan con una zona de exposición, en la que destacan una luminosa pared de lentejuelas y un cubo negro central de inspiración minimalista.

Les créateurs de ce projet devaient imaginer un *show-room* qui proposerait un espace commun de réunion pour les commerciaux spécialisés en meubles de bureau, ainsi qu'un espace de travail pour les créateurs de la marque et de Se'lux, sa filiale spécialisée dans l'éclairage. Les installations sont dotées d'un espace d'exposition, où l'on remarque un mur lumineux de paillettes et un cube noir central d'inspiration minimaliste.

L'incarico accettato dai designer di questo progetto consisteva in una *showroom* volta a creare un'area comune di riunione per i rappresentanti commerciali specializzati in arredo per ufficio nonché uno spazio di lavoro per i progettisti della marca e di Se'lux, la rispettiva divisione di illuminazione. Gli allestimenti presentano un'area espositiva, in cui spiccano una parete luminosa di lustrini e un cubo nero centrale, d'ispirazione minimalista.

Graft | Berlin
Sci Fi, Comic-Con International
San Diego, CA, USA | 2005

As part of a comics and pop culture fair, design lab Graft created this stand for the Sci Fi Channel. The structure, which recalls the form of a large eel, includes an installation of LED systems that creates a play of projections against the variously sloping walls. It also features an area with multimedia content and three LCD screens that reveal the channel's content for the upcoming season.

Im Rahmen der Messe für Comics und Popkultur entwarf das Designlabor Graft diesen Stand für den Fernsehkanal Sci Fi Channel. Die formale Struktur, die einen riesigen Adler evoziert, besitzt eine LED-Installation, mit der ein Spiel von Projektionen auf die Wände in ihren verschiedenen Neigungswinkeln geschaffen wurde. Es gibt auch einen Multimedia-Bereich und drei LCD-Bildschirme, die bereits die Inhalte zeigen, welche der Kanal für die kommende Saison geplant hat.

En el marco de una feria de cómics y cultura pop, el laboratorio de diseño Graft diseñó este *stand* para Sci Fi Channel. La estructura, que evoca la forma de una anguila gigante, incorpora una instalación de sistemas LED que crea un juego de proyecciones en las paredes, de distintas inclinaciones. También dispone de un área con contenido multimedia y tres pantallas LCD que adelantan los contenidos del canal para la próxima temporada.

Dans le cadre d'un salon de bande dessinée et de culture pop, le laboratoire de design Graft a conçu ce *stand* pour Sci Fi Channel. La structure, dont la forme évoque une anguille géante, est équipée d'une installation de systèmes LED qui créent un jeu de projections sur les murs inclinés selon différents angles. Elle est également dotée d'un espace multimédia et de trois écrans LCD qui présentent les programmes de la chaîne pour la prochaine saison.

Nell'ambito di un salone dei fumetti e della cultura pop, lo studio di design Graft ha curato il progetto di questo *stand* per lo Sci Fi Channel. La struttura, rievocante la forma di un'anguilla gigante, possiede un impianto di sistemi LED atto a creare un gioco di proiezioni sulle pareti variamente inclinate. È disponibile, altresì, un'area multimediale e tre schermi LCD che presenta un'anteprima dei contenuti del canale per la prossima stagione.

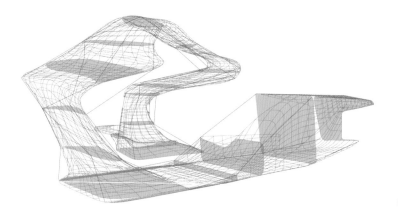

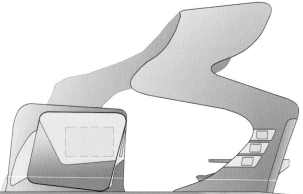

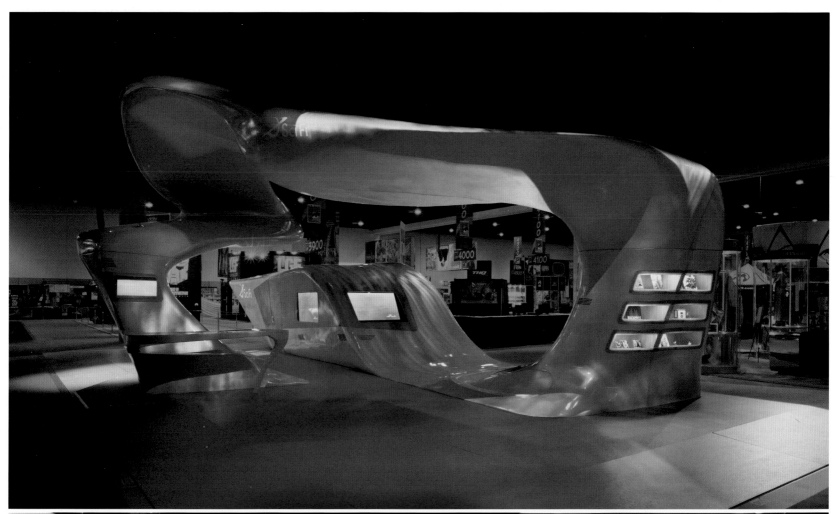

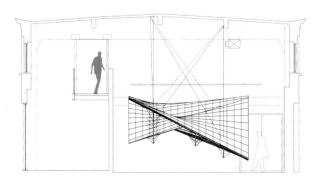

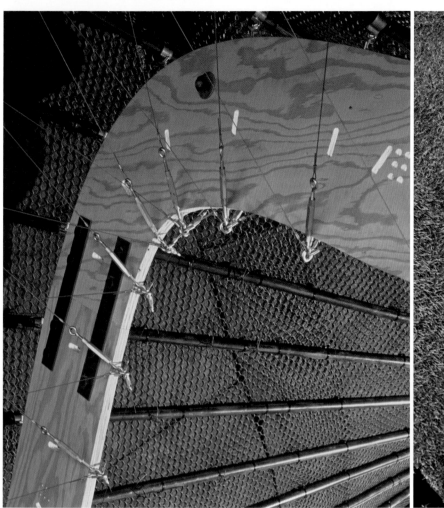

An **undulating and omnipresent** grass box was the indisputable star of this trade fair that aimed to investigate our cultural relations with this geographic feature and urban resource. The way it hangs suspended nearly 1,000 square feet from the surface from fine metallic cables emphasizes its extreme slenderness and, according to the architects, indicates the dichotomy between its organic nature and eminently artificial character.

Ein gewelltes, allgegenwärtiges Rasenfeld ist der unstrittige Protagonist dieser Schau, die versucht, unsere kulturelle Beziehung zu dieser Art von Geländeunebenheit und urbaner Ressource zu erforschen. Indem fast 100 Quadratmeter dieser Oberfläche durch feine Metallkabel aufgehängt wurden, sollte deutlich gemacht werden, wie hauchdünn sie ist. Den Architekten zufolge wird so der Doppelcharakter zwischen organischer Natur und ausgesprochen künstlichem Charakter gezeigt.

Un ondulante y omnipresente trozo de césped es el indiscutible protagonista de esta muestra que trata de indagar en nuestra relación cultural con este accidente geográfico y recurso urbanístico. Al suspender casi 100 m² de esta superficie mediante finos cables metálicos, queda de manifiesto su extrema delgadez y, según los arquitectos, se señala la dicotomía entre su naturaleza orgánica y su carácter eminentemente artificial.

Un cadre ondulant et omniprésent de pelouse est la vedette incontestée de cette exposition qui explore notre relation culturelle avec cet élément, à la fois accident géographique et solution d'aménagement urbain. En suspendant cette tenture de presque 100 m² à de fins câbles métalliques, les architectes mettent en évidence sa finesse extrême et veulent attirer l'attention sur la dichotomie entre sa nature organique et son caractère éminemment artificiel.

Un tappeto erboso ondulante e onnipresente è il protagonista indiscusso di questa mostra tesa a esaminare il rapporto culturale che ci lega a questo elemento geografico e risorsa urbanistica. La sospensione di quasi 100 m² di tale superficie, avvalendosi di sottili cavi metallici, ne evidenzia l'estrema sottigliezza nonché, a detta degli architetti, la dicotomia tra la sua natura organica e il suo carattere eminentemente artificiale.

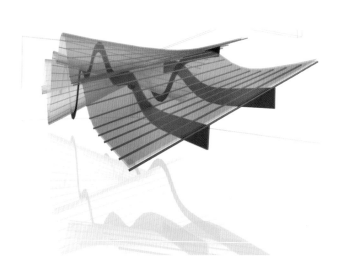

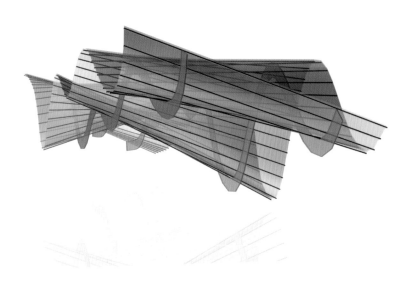

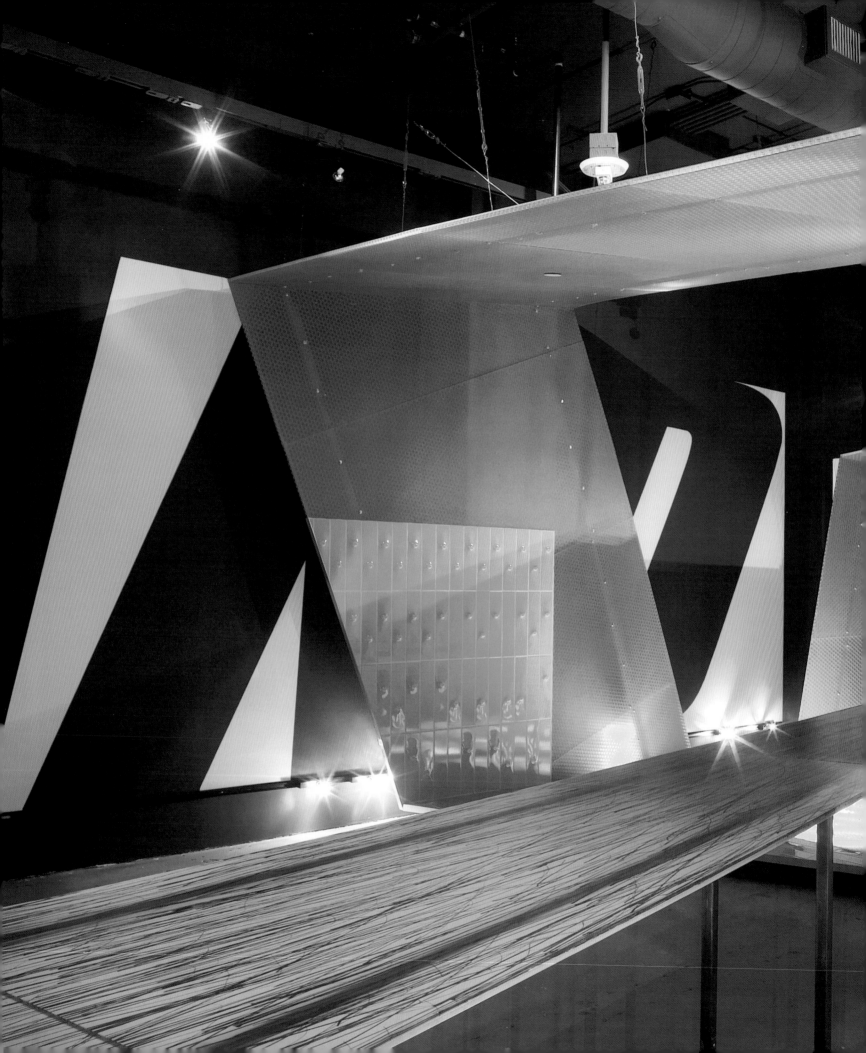

Griffin Enright Architects | Los Angeles
(Wide) Band, NeoCon West
Los Angeles, CA, USA | 2006

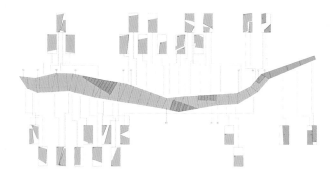

Covering an area of 5,300 square feet, this installation is the result of a commission by the magazine *Interior Design* and NeoCon West to design a space where attendees of different conferences can consult their emails, get together or just enjoy a break from their professional activity. With an orange surface that folds over on itself, the space is surrounded by the panel that lends the project its name.

Diese Installation auf einer Fläche von etwas mehr als 500 Quadratmetern Fläche ist das Ergebnis eines Auftrags, den die Zeitschrift *Interior Design* und NeoCon West dem Architekten erteilten, nämlich einen Raum zu konzipieren, in dem die Teilnehmer der verschiedenen Konferenzen ihre E-Mails abrufen, sich zum Gespräch treffen oder auch kurz von ihren beruflichen Aktivitäten ausruhen könnten. Der Raum mit einer orangen Oberfläche ist von dem Schriftzug des Projekts umgeben.

Con algo más de 500 m² de superficie, esta instalación es el resultado del encargo realizado a los arquitectos por la revista *Interior Design* y por NeoCon West: concebir un espacio en el que los asistentes a las conferencias pudieran consultar el correo electrónico, reunirse para hablar o descansar un momento de la actividad profesional. Con una superficie naranja que se pliega sobre sí misma, el espacio está rodeado por el panel que da nombre al proyecto.

Avec plus de 500 m² de surface, cette installation est le résultat de la commande que le magazine *Interior Design* et NeoCon West ont passée aux architectes : concevoir un espace pour que les participants à différentes conférences puissent consulter leurs e-mails, se réunir pour parler ou se reposer un moment de leurs activités professionnelles. Une surface orange se replie sur elle-même et l'espace est entouré par un panneau qui donne son nom au projet.

Con 500 m² di superficie, questo allestimento è stato commissionato dalla rivista *Interior Design* e NeoCon West; si tratta di uno spazio in cui i partecipanti a varie conferenze possono consultare la propria *e-mail*, riunirsi per conversare oppure concedersi un attimo di sosta nel corso della loro attività professionale. Grazie a una superficie di color arancione pieghevole, l'ambiente viene circondato dal pannello che dà il nome al progetto.

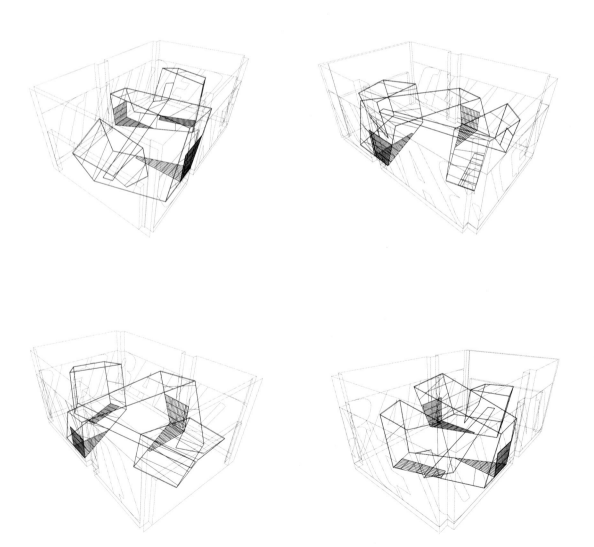

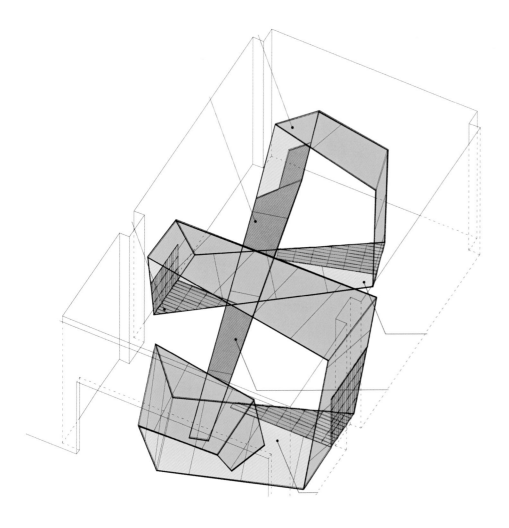

Hackenbroich Architekten | Berlin
The Traffic of Clouds, No event
Berlin, Germany | 2007

Made in collaboration with Jan Christensen, the artist responsible for the mural, this unusual installation is remarkable for its use of wooden strips, reminiscent of giant ice-cream sticks, interwoven along the length of the space and with no connecting element. Collaboration between the architects and the artist made it possible to share different methodologies, resulting in an impressive visual effect.

Diese ungewöhnliche Installation, die unter Mitarbeit von Jan Christensen, von dem das Wandbild stammt, entstand, sticht durch den Einsatz von Holz-latten hervor. Sie wirken wie riesige Eis-Stiele und sind über den gesamten Raum ohne eine Verbindung, die sie zusammenhalten würde, miteinander verwoben. Die Zusammenarbeit der Architekten mit dem Künstler erlaubte es, verschiedene Methoden zu kombinieren – dabei kamen beeindruckende visuelle Effekte heraus.

Realizada en colaboración con Jan Christensen, autor del mural, esta curiosa instalación destaca por el empleo de listones de madera que, como palos de helados gigantes, se entretejen a lo largo del espacio sin ningún elemento conector que los ensamble. La colaboración entre los arquitectos y el artista permitió la puesta en común de distintas metodologías, con un resultado de impresionantes efectos visuales.

Cette curieuse installation réalisée en collaboration avec Jan Christensen, l'auteur de l'œuvre exposée au mur, se distingue par l'utilisation de pièces de bois qui, comme des bâtonnets de glace géants, s'entrecroisent tout le long de l'espace sans qu'aucun élément les relie entre elles. La collaboration des architectes et de l'artiste a permis de mettre en commun des méthodologies différentes, ce qui a donné des effets visuels impressionnants.

Allestita in collaborazione con Jan Christensen, autore del murale, questa singolare struttura spicca grazie all'uso di asticelle lignee che, a guisa di giganti bastoni di gelati, s'intrecciano in tutto lo spazio senza alcun elemento connettore in grado di assemblarli. La collaborazione tra gli architetti e l'artista ha consentito di accorpare varie metodologie, il cui risultato sono degli effetti visivi di grande impatto.

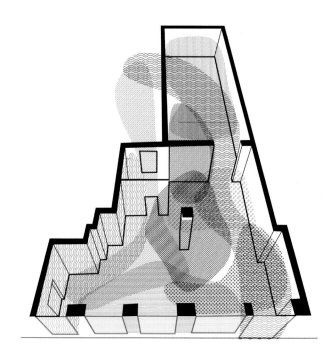
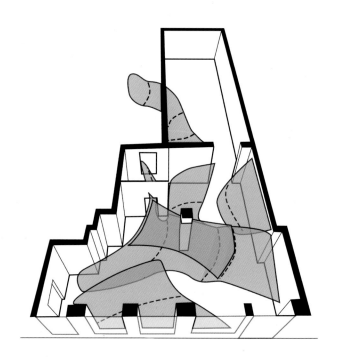

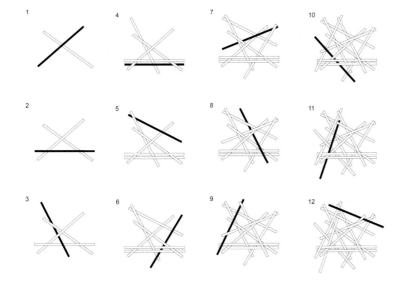

JSA Design Development | Mexico City
Showroom Piacere 3, No event
Mexico City, Mexico | 2006

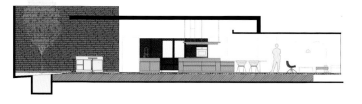

The design of this furniture showroom stands out for the 'negative' simulation carried out on the casing the space comprises. The white tones and cold lighting of former years is here replaced by gray graphite shadows with the predominance of amber light. The effect the designers were aiming for was a dynamic and kinetic invitation to explore the installation at leisure.

Blickfang bei der Gestaltung dieses Showrooms von Innenmobiliar ist, dass die Umhüllung, die den Raum umgibt, quasi in Negativform simuliert wird. Von Weißtönen und kalter Beleuchtung ging man zu grauen Grafit-Tönen und mehr amberfarbenem Licht über. Angestrebt wurde eine dynamische, kinetische Wirkung, die man als Einladung verstehen könnte, die Installation in Ruhe zu durchlaufen.

El diseño de este *showroom* de mobiliario de cocinas y baños destaca por la simulación, llevada a cabo «en negativo», del envoltorio que abarca el espacio. De los tonos blancos y la iluminación en frío de otras ediciones se pasa a las sombras grisáceas del grafito, con el predominio de una luz de color ámbar. Se buscó un efecto dinámico, kinético, que invitara a recorrer la instalación tranquilamente.

Ce *show-room* de meubles de cuisine et de salle de bains est remarquable pour la simulation « en négatif » de l'enveloppe de l'espace. Les tons blancs et la lumière froide des éditions précédentes ont laissé place aux ombres grises du graphite, dominées par une lumière ambrée. On a recherché un effet dynamique qui invite à visiter l'installation en toute tranquillité.

Il progetto di questa *showroom* di arredamenti di bagni e cucine spicca grazie alla simulazione, realizzata «in negativo», dell'involucro che cinge lo spazio. Le tonalità bianche e l'illuminazione fredda delle edizioni scorse, cedono il posto a ombre grigiastre della grafite, in cui predomina una luce di colore ambra. Si è ricercato un effetto dinamico e, cinetico, che inducesse a percorrere tranquillamente tale allestimento.

Llongueras Clotet Arquitectes | Barcelona
Technal, Construmat
Barcelona, Spain | 2007

The structure of this stand recalls an enormous shiny prism emerging from a black package like a jewel in a half-opened case. Five black boxes arranged at varying heights create five distinct platforms on which five different displays of the brand's products are presented. This alludes to the cohesive spirit with which Technal aims to bring together professionals from the world of construction.

Die Struktur dieses Stands ist so angelegt, dass sie an ein enormes glänzendes Prisma denken lässt, das — wie ein Schmuckstück in einem halb geöffneten Etui — aus einer schwarzen Umhüllung herausragt. Fünf schwarze Kästen in unterschiedlicher Höhe schaffen fünf unterschiedliche Szenerien, in denen fünf verschiedene Darbietungen der Marke präsentiert werden; dies spielt auf den Geist an, unter dem Technal die Fachleute des Bauwesens unter seinem Namen verbinden möchte.

La estructura de este *stand* viene a evocar un enorme prisma brillante que sobresale de un envoltorio negro, como una joya en un estuche entreabierto. Cinco cajas negras dispuestas a diferentes alturas crean cinco escenarios distintos, en los que se presentan cinco muestras de la marca; ello alude al espíritu aglutinador con el que Technal pretende aunar a los profesionales del mundo de la construcción bajo su firma.

La structure de ce *stand* évoque un énorme prisme brillant qui dépasse d'un coffret noir, comme un bijou précieux dans un écrin entrouvert. Cinq boîtes noires placées à différentes hauteurs forment cinq plateaux, où sont présentés cinq échantillons de la marque. Cette mise en scène fait référence à l'esprit de Technal, qui souhaite réunir les professionnels du monde de la construction sous sa signature.

La struttura di questo *stand* rievoca un prisma brillante di grandi proporzioni, sporgente da un involucro nero al pari di un gioiello in un cofanetto socchiuso. Cinque scatole nere, sistemate a varie altezze, danno vita a cinque scenari diversi, in cui vengono allestite cinque mostre diverse del marchio; il tutto, allude allo spirito accorpante con cui Technal intende raggruppare gli addetti ai lavori del settore edile sotto la sua firma.

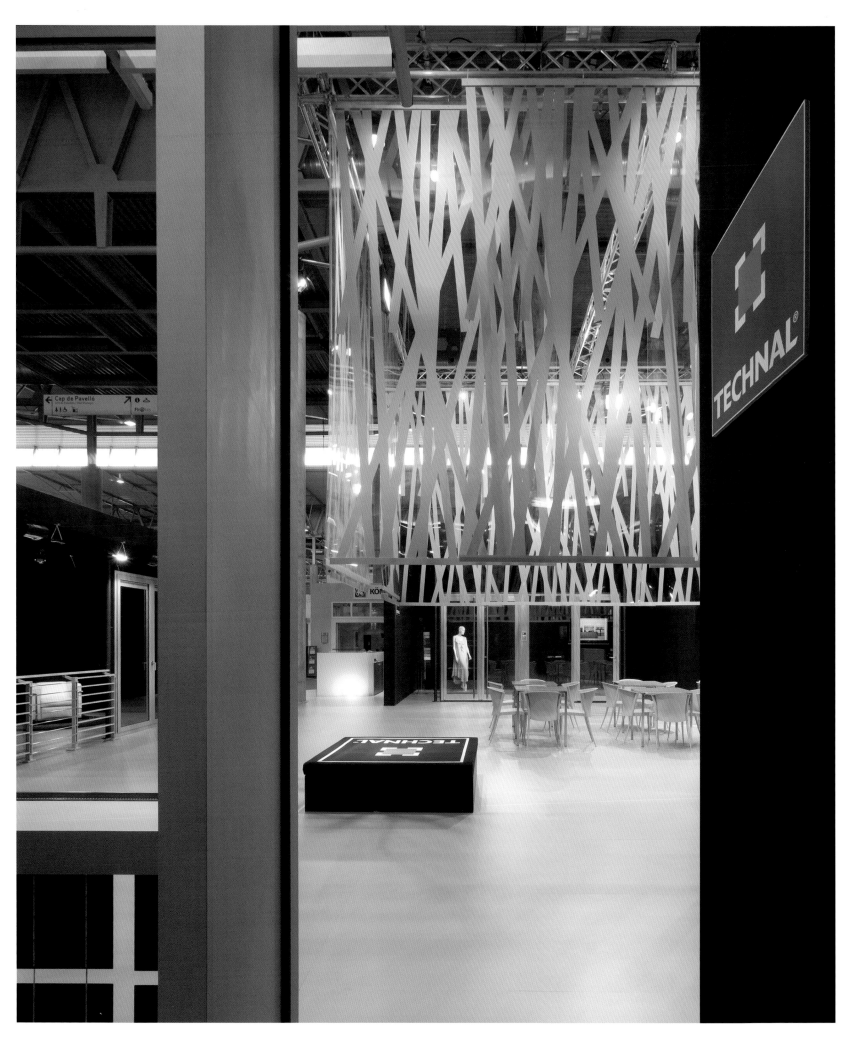

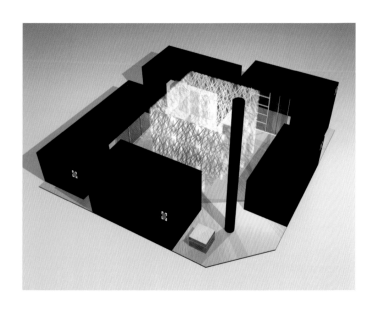

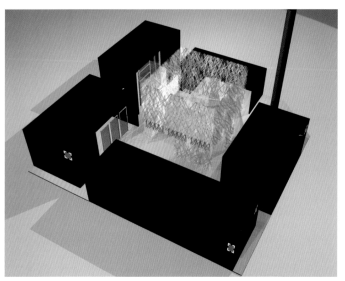

Marita Madden Merchandise | Port Melbourne
The French National Collection, Life in Style
Melbourne, Australia | 2007

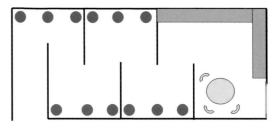

THE FRENCH NATIONAL COLLECTION THE LOUVRE PARIS

M.
Marita
Madden
Merchandise

The purpose of this intervention was to create an attention-grabbing exhibition space in the context of a trade fair in one of the world's oldest trade-fair centers. The idea behind the stand was to offer visitors a chance to see the art works on sale in a setting that would resemble the one where they would be positioned following purchase. The graphic design and corporate image were done in collaboration with Ty Bukewitsch from The Envelope Group studio.

Ziel dieses Beitrags zu einer Ausstellung in einem der ältesten Messepavillons der Welt war es, einen wirklich aufmerksamkeitserregenden Ausstellungsraum zu schaffen. Die zum Verkauf angebotenen Kunstobjekte sollten dem Besucher in einem Umfeld präsentiert werden, das dem Ort ähnelte, an dem die Werke nach ihrem Kauf aufgestellt würden. Die Grafiken und das Corporate Image wurden in Zusammenarbeit mit Ty Bukewitsch von The Envelope Group gestaltet.

El objetivo de esta intervención fue la creación de un espacio de exhibición llamativo dentro del contexto de una muestra situada en uno de los pabellones feriales más antiguos del mundo. El puesto debía brindar al visitante la posibilidad de ver los objetos artísticos en venta en un entorno que se asemejara al lugar en que éstos se ubicarían después de su adquisición. Los gráficos y la imagen corporativa fueron realizados en colaboración con Ty Bukewitsch, del estudio The Envelope Group.

L'objectif de cette intervention était de créer un espace d'exposition séduisant à l'intérieur d'un salon situé dans l'un des pavillons d'exposition les plus anciens au monde. Il devait présenter aux visiteurs des objets artistiques dans un décor similaire à celui qui allait les accueillir après leur acquisition. Les graphismes et l'image d'entreprise ont été réalisés en collaboration avec Ty Bukewitsch, du studio The Envelope Group.

Lo scopo di questo intervento è stato quello di creare uno spazio espositivo attraente nel contesto di una mostra situata in uno dei padiglioni di fiera più antichi del mondo. L'idea è stata quella di offrire al visitante la possibilità di vedere gli oggetti artistici in vendita in un ambiente il più possibile simile al luogo in cui si troverebbero dopo il loro acquisto. La grafica e l'immagine aziendale sono state realizzate in collaborazione con Ty Bukewitsch, dello studio The Envelope Group.

IV

Marita Madden Merchan

VINYL LETTERING APPLIED TO MATCH PANTONE 166U AND SOLID BLACK
THE FRENCH NATIONAL COLLECTION THE LOUVRE PARIS
THE FRENCH NATIONAL COLLECTION THE LOUVRE PARIS
EXIT
BACK ELEVATION

THE FRENCH NATIONAL COLLECTION THE LOUVRE PARIS
M
Marita Madden Merchandise
THE FRENCH NATIONAL COLLECTION THE LOUVRE PARIS
VINYL LETTERING APPLIED TO MATCH PANTONE 240U AND SOLID BLACK

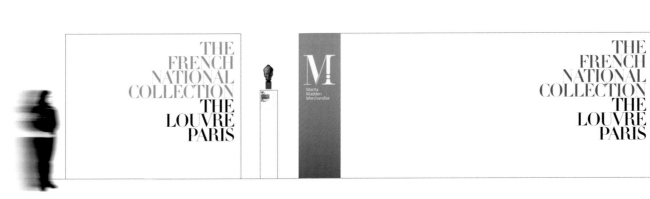

Marita
Madden
Merchandise

Martínez y Soler Arquitectos | Granada
Francisco Ayala Exhibition, Royal Hospital
Granada, Spain | 2006

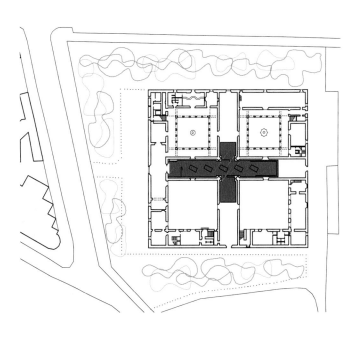

Celebrating the centenary of the writer's birth, this exhibition brings together a number of documents and objects related with the life and work of Francisco Ayala. With the route divided into periods of his career, it makes the most of its formal environment in a 16th century building. The exhibition consists, among other elements, of unbroken floating parquet wooden floors, 10-foot high perimeter walls.

Anlässlich des 100. Geburtstags Francisco Ayalas trägt diese Präsentation ein Konvolut von Dokumenten und Objekten zusammen, die mit Leben und Werk des Schriftstellers zu tun haben. Der Rundgang gliedert sich entsprechend den Etappen im Werdegang des Autors. Dabei profitiert die Ausstellung von der feierlichen Atmosphäre der Umgebung, einem Gebäude aus dem 16. Jahrhundert. Die Ausstellung besteht unter anderem aus einem durchgängigen schwimmenden Parkettboden und drei Meter hohen Elementen, die alles umschließen.

Con motivo del centenario del escritor, esta exposición recopila un conjunto de documentos y objetos relacionados con la vida y la obra de Francisco Ayala. Dividiendo el recorrido en las etapas de la trayectoria del creador, la muestra saca provecho de la solemnidad del entorno —un edificio del siglo XVI—; dicha exposición está compuesta, entre otros elementos, por un suelo continuo de parqué flotante y unos paramentos perimetrales de 3 m de altura.

À l'occasion du centenaire de Francisco Ayala, cette exposition rassemble des documents et objets liés à la vie et l'œuvre de l'écrivain. Le parcours est divisé en plusieurs parties correspondant à la trajectoire de l'auteur, et l'exposition tire parti de la solennité de l'environnement — un bâtiment du XVIe siècle. Elle se compose, entre autres éléments, d'un sol continu en parquet flottant et de parements de 3 mètres de hauteur sur le périmètre.

In occasione del centesimo compleanno di Francisco Ayala, questa mostra accomuna documenti e oggetti legati alla vita e all'opera di questo scrittore. Nell'articolarne il percorso in base alle varie fasi della sua carriera, la mostra sfrutta il tono solenne del palazzo del XVI secolo ove è stata allestita utilizzando, tra l'altro, elementi quali un pavimento continuo di parquet galleggiante e paramenti perimetrali alti 3 m.

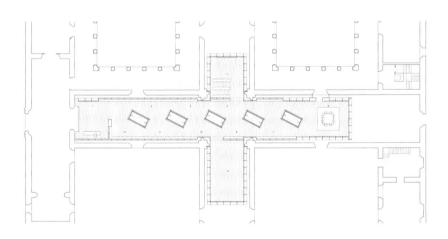

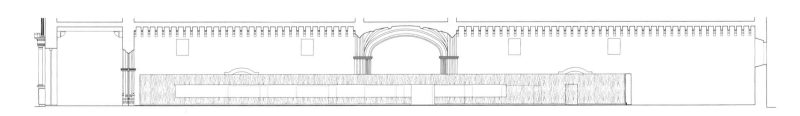

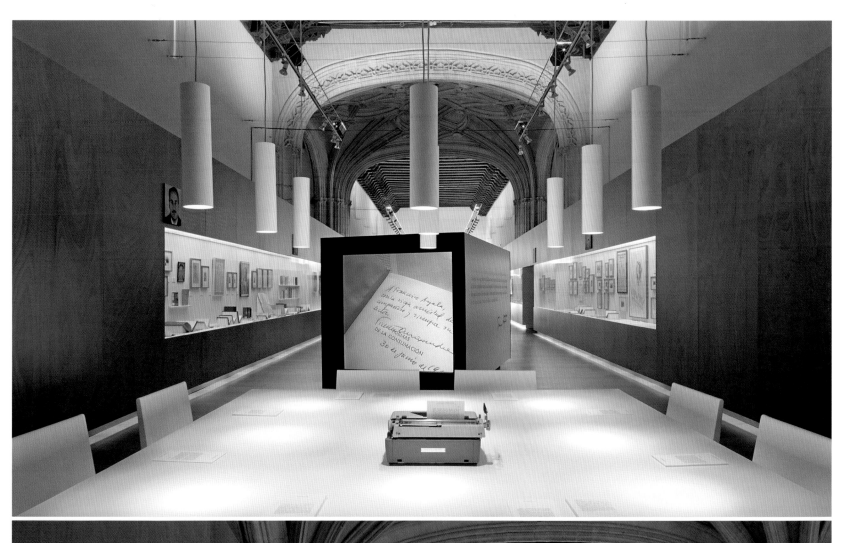

1916-1917
Durante algunos meses de este curso, el primero de su Bachillerato, fue alumno del colegio de los Padres Escolapios. En los niveles anteriores de enseñanza había

asistido al Colegio de Niñas Nobles y al Colegio Calderón.

1918-1921
Estudia en el Instituto General y Técnico de Granada.

1922
Problemas ec obligan a la f de Francisco trasladarse a En esta ciuda el bachillerat Instituto San

EL DEFENSOR DE GRANADA

濕地世界
北地苔原

LIVING WETLANDS
FROZEN NORTH

在極北的苔原並無樹木，卻佈滿濕地。每當夏天降臨，地面冰雪融解，仍是冰封的地底卻把雪水留住，形成濕地。

In the far north is a vast treeless expanse, called the tundra, which is rich in wetlands. When the snow melts in summer, the water does not drain away because the ground below stays frozen.

候鳥的遷徙
BIRD MIGRATION

旅行者
TRAVELLERS

WHIMBREL

Met Studio Design | London
Wetland Discovery Centre, Wetland Park
Hong Kong, China | 2008

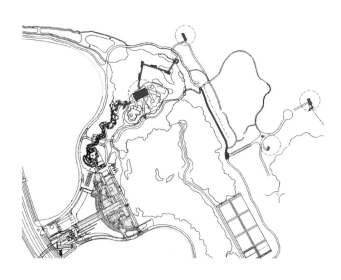

The design of this permanent exhibition, part of the world's biggest wetland ecological park aimed mainly at being spectacular. The galleries take visitors through very distinct spaces such as a polar environment, a tropical landscape and a wetland in Hong Kong, as well as a fake television set. The combination of information panels, stuffed animals and crocodiles makes it extremely attractive.

Die Gestaltung dieser auf eine spektakuläre Wirkung angelegten Dauerausstellung fügt sich in den weltgrößten Ökopark mit Feuchtbiotopen ein. Galerien leiten den Besucher durch so unterschiedliche Räume wie ein Polargebiet, eine tropische Sumpflandschaft und ein Feuchtbiotop, wie man es in Hong Kong findet, sowie in einer fingierten Fernsehkulisse. Die Kombination aus Infotafeln, Tierpräparaten und echten Krokodilen wirbt auf attraktive Art für ihr Anliegen.

El diseño de esta exposición permanente, emplazada en el parque ecológico de humedales más grande del mundo, tuvo como principal objetivo la espectacularidad. Las galerías hacen que el visitante transite por espacios tan distintos como un ambiente polar, un pantano tropical y un humedal de Hong Kong, así como un falso plató de televisión. La combinación de paneles informativos, animales disecados y cocodrilos se convierte en un reclamo realmente atractivo.

Cette exposition permanente du plus grand parc écologique de zones humides du monde a pour objectif principal d'être spectaculaire. Ses galeries font passer le public par des espaces complètement différents les uns des autres, comme un paysage polaire, un marais tropical et une zone humide de Hong Kong, ainsi qu'un faux plateau de télévision. La combinaison de panneaux d'information, d'animaux disséqués et de vrais crocodiles se révèle particulièrement intéressante.

Questa esposizione permanente, inserita nel parco ecologico di zone umide più grande del mondo, ha raggiunto il suo obiettivo di spettacolarità. Infatti, le sue gallerie invitano il visitatore a percorrere spazi diametralmente opposti come un ambiente polare, una palude tropicale e una zona umida di Hong Kong nonché uno studio televisivo falso. La combinazione di pannelli informativi, animali imbalsamati e coccodrilli produce un forte richiamo sulla gente.

泛洪森林

亞馬遜河每年都會泛濫，淹浸超過10萬平方公里的森林，面積比100個香港還要大，河水水位可達9至12米深，使不少樹木部分浸在水中數月之久。魚群在樹林中游弋，樹上掉下來的果實讓牠們大快朵頤；牠們同時也為樹木傳播種子。

亞馬遜河是逾3,000種罕有水生物種的家園，包括巨型水獺和兩種當地原生海豚。

FLOODED FOREST

The River Amazon floods over 100,000 square kilo[m] forest every year - an area 100 times larger than H[o] The water can rise up to 9 to 12 metres, partially submerging the trees for many months. Fishes swi[m] amongst the trees. Some eat fruit fallen into the w[ater] aid the tree's seed dispersal.

The Amazon is home to over 3,000 rare species of life including the Giant Otter and two native dolph[in]

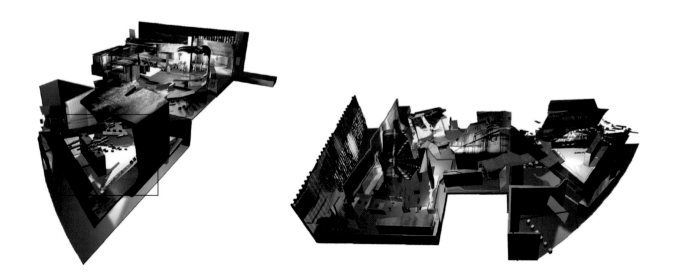

消逝中的森林
DISAPPEARING FORESTS

Nosinger | Tokyo
Techtile Exhibition, University of Tokyo
Tokyo, Japan | 2007

Focused on the integration of tactile design and the promotion of the latest technologies in this area, the development of this exhibition included the collaboration of Yasuaki Kakehi and Masashi Nakatani. Evoking the sensory experience of touching an ice cube, it is an attempt to create icicles and elongated, conical ice formations made from wrapped plastic. The cost of the exhibition was just $1.50 per square foot.

An der Entwicklung der Ausstellung, die auf die Integration von taktilem Design und auf die Präsentation aktueller Technologien abzielt, waren Yasuaki Kakehi und Masashi Nakatani beteiligt. Grundidee war es, die sinnliche Erfahrung, die sich bei der Berührung eines Eiswürfels einstellt, wachzurufen. So kreierte man für diese Präsentation Eiszapfen — lange, konische Formationen aus Verpackungsmaterial. Der Kostenaufwand für die Ausstellung beträgt rund 10 Euro pro Quadratmeter.

Enfocada a la integración del diseño táctil y a dar a conocer las últimas tecnologías en este ámbito, esta exposición se ha desarrollado con la colaboración de Yasuaki Kakehi y Masashi Nakatani. Con idea de evocar la experiencia sensorial de tocar un cubo de hielo, esta muestra es un intento de crear carámbanos, formaciones de hielo largas y cónicas, hechos con plástico para embalaje. El mínimo coste de la muestra ronda los 10 euros por metro cuadrado.

Yasuaki Kakehi et Masashi Nakatani ont participé à l'élaboration de cette exposition, qui a pour but de présenter au public le design tactile et les dernières technologies employées dans ce domaine. Pour évoquer l'expérience sensorielle que l'on a lorsqu'on touche un glaçon, on a essayé ici de créer des stalactites, des formations de glaces allongées et coniques, à l'aide de plastique d'emballage. L'exposition a été réalisée pour un coût modique d'environ 10 euros par m².

Nell'allestire quest'esposizione, incentrata sull'integrazione del design tattile e tesa a far conoscere le ultime tecnologie in questo settore, ci si è avvalsi della collaborazione di Yasuaki Kakehi e di Masashi Nakatani. La mostra, che evoca l'esperienza sensoriale di toccare un cubo di ghiaccio, rappresenta un tentativo di creare ghiaccioli, formazioni di ghiaccio allungate e coniche, fatti con plastica da imballo. Il costo minimo della mostra si attesta sui 10 euros/m².

TECHTILE

Paolo Cesaretti | Milan
Coop Stand, ECR Europe Forum & Marketplace
Milan, Italy | 2007

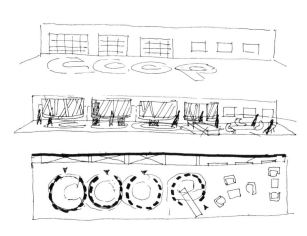

The project for this exhibition was conceived from the start on the principle of simplicity in design. ECR's institutional colors, i.e., white and red, are combined in all the areas of the site. The simple strips that fall from the ceiling to form circular spaces create exhibition cubicles, while the large wall in the background reflects the thematic symbol of the values of union, one of the main claims of the supermarket company that publicizes it.

Bei der Konzeption dieser Ausstellung regierte von Anfang an das Prinzip der Einfachheit. Die Kombination der Farben des Unternehmens ECR – Weiß und Rot – taucht auf allen Oberflächen auf. Die einfachen Streifen, die von der Decke in Rundformen hängen und Raum bildende Wirkung haben, formen Ausstellungsnischen, während die weite Rückwand die Thematik – Einigkeit und Zusammengehörigkeit – symbolisiert, eines der Hauptaushängeschilder der beworbenen Supermarkt-Kette.

El proyecto de esta muestra se concibió siguiendo el principio de sencillez en el diseño. Los colores institucionales de ECR (el blanco y el rojo) se combinan en todas las superficies del recinto. Las tiras simples que cuelgan del techo para formar espacios circulares crean cubículos de exposición. La amplia pared del fondo evoca el símbolo temático de los valores de unión, uno de los principales reclamos de la firma de supermercados que se publicita.

Le projet de cette exposition a été conçu dès le départ avec une grande simplicité. Les couleurs institutionnelles d'ECR (le blanc et le rouge) se combinent sur toutes les surfaces de l'espace. Les bandes qui tombent du plafond pour former des espaces circulaires créent des cubiculaires d'exposition, et le grand mur du fond évoque le symbole thématique des valeurs d'union, l'un des piliers de la communication de cette chaîne de supermarchés.

Questa mostra è stata progettata, sin dalle sue fasi iniziali, nel segno della semplicità. I colori istituzionali della società ECR (bianco e rosso) si combinano in tutte le superfici di tale spazio mentre le strisce, dall'aspetto semplice, che pendono dal soffitto per formare spazi circolari, danno vita a zone espositive. L'estesa parete in fondo evoca il simbolo tematico dell'unione, una delle maggiori attrazioni della società di supermercati pubblicizzata.

Paolo Cesaretti | Milan
Made in Italy Files, Domitian's Stadium
Rome, Italy | 2007

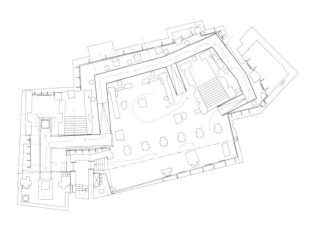

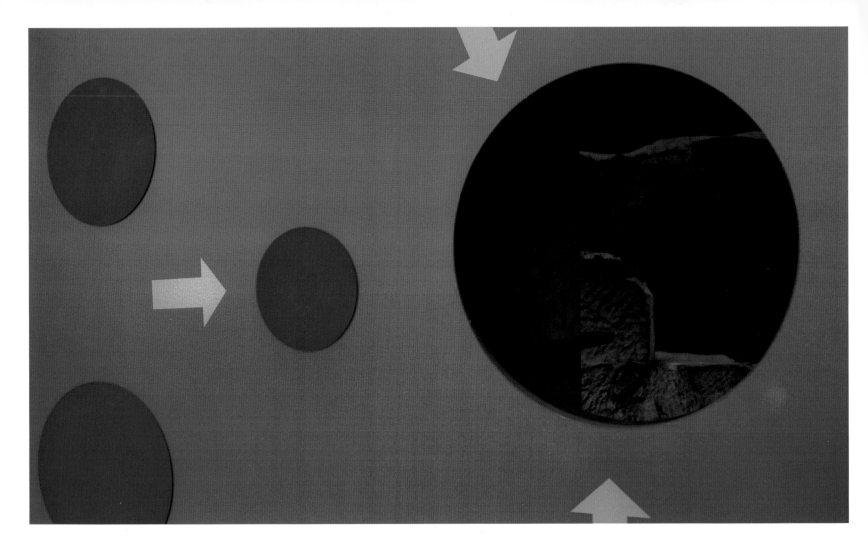

This exhibition is located in Rome's fascinating Domitian's Stadium, which demonstrates the organizers' initial intention to establish a contrast between the brightly colored contemporary materials and the archeological stone treasures which surround them. A large red vertical panel leads the way through the exhibition and is its calling card along with the suspended footbridge, which visitors cross.

Die Ausstellung befindet sich in dem faszinierenden römischen Stadion des Domitian; damit war von Anfang an klar, dass es sich anböte, einen Kontrast zwischen den aktuellen Materialien in glänzenden Tönen und dem archäologischen Schatz aus Stein außen herum herzustellen. Eine große senkrechte Tafel, die die Funktion einer Visitenkarte der Ausstellung hat, markiert zusammen mit dem hängenden Laufsteg den Rundgang durch die Ausstellung.

La exposición se ubica en el fascinante estadio romano de Domiciano, con lo que desde el principio quedó clara la conveniencia de establecer un contraste entre los materiales contemporáneos, de tonos brillantes, y el tesoro arqueológico de piedra que los iba a rodear. Un gran panel vertical rojo marca el recorrido de la muestra y actúa como carta de presentación de la exposición, junto con la pasarela colgante por la que transitan los visitantes.

Cette exposition a été installée dans le magnifique cirque romain Domitien. Dès le début, il est apparu très clairement qu'il convenait de jouer sur le contraste entre les matériaux contemporains de couleurs vives et le trésor archéologique en pierre qui allait leur servir de décor. Un grand panneau vertical rouge trace le parcours de l'exposition et fait office de carte de visite, avec la passerelle suspendue sur laquelle passent les visiteurs.

L'esposizione è stata allestita nello stadio romano di Domiziano; il che ha evidenziato chiaramente, sin dall'inizio, l'opportunità di stabilire un contrasto tra i materiali contemporanei, dai toni brillanti, e il tesoro archeologico in pietra che avrebbe fatto loro da cornice. Un grande pannello verticale rosso segna il percorso della mostra e ne svolge altresì la funzione di biglietto di presentazione unitamente alla passerella pensile su cui la stessa si svolge.

MADE IN ITALY FILES

Testo abcde frg
shruv mfjefwd adeffef
dvggf dffrgrg www mcckel

Testo abcde frg
shruv mfjefwd adeffef
dvggf dffrgrg www mcckel

Testo abcde frg
shruv mfjefwd adeffef
dvggf dffrgrg www mcckef

242

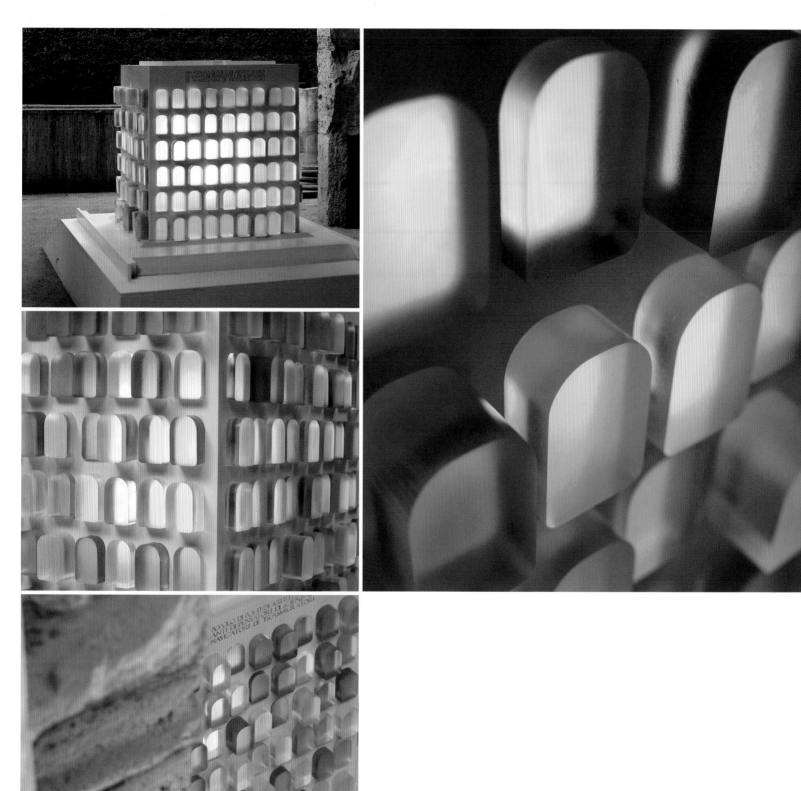

العوالم المفقودة

LOST WORLDS

مجموعة المعارض هذه وحولها منطقة كبيرة منطلقة من
الطبيعة من عينها الظاهر كائنات كبيرة نتة من
من خلالها... فتتح وتشرت وتتشرت بعائن تستطين
تواتي مقاييس متسلسل أشكال الحياة العربية في تأملين
بعيدة متضامنة نثوره من وجهة العالم الانقراض موجودات
ان الطبيعة في حياة خليف خصيصة من الطبيعة... فجأة
والحيوانات من شروق الأرض في أسوأ التغييرات التكاثلية
في يومنا هذا وألول نكثر منها حظر نظرة الانقراض
ونطاولها محدد تحت خلية.

Pentagram | London
Lost Worlds, London Natural History Museum
Doha, Qatar | 2005

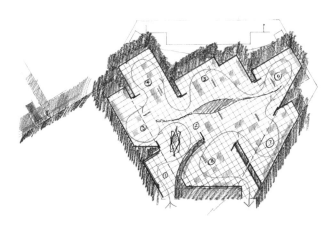

This **temporary exhibition** of meteorites and the fossils of dinosaurs and other extinct animals drew a record-breaking number of visitors and was universally acclaimed for its quality. Designed to attract children and adults alike, the exhibition aimed to illustrate the fragility of our ecosystems. Pentagram underlined this idea with a design that created dramatic ambiances and highlighted the individual beauty of each piece on display.

Diese temporäre Ausstellung von Meteoriten sowie Fossilien von Dinosauriern und ausgestorbenen Tierarten verzeichnete einen Zuschauerrekord und erhielt weltweit Anerkennung. Ihre Gestaltung, die die Aufmerksamkeit auf die Fragilität unserer Ökosysteme lenkte, sollte sowohl Kinder wie Erwachsene ansprechen. Pentagram unterstrich diesen Gedanken mit einem Design, das eine dramatische Atmosphäre hervorbrachte und die individuelle Schönheit jedes einzelnen Exponats hervorhob.

Esta exposición temporal de meteoritos y fósiles de dinosaurios y animales extinguidos obtuvo un récord de visitantes y fue aclamada en todo el mundo por su calidad. Diseñada para atraer la atención tanto de niños como de adultos, la muestra trataba de llamar la atención sobre la fragilidad de nuestros ecosistemas. Pentagram subrayó esta idea con un diseño que creaba ambientes impactantes y resaltaba la belleza individual de cada una de las piezas expuestas.

Cette exposition temporaire de météorites et de fossiles de dinosaures et d'animaux disparus a attiré un nombre record de visiteurs et a été acclamée dans le monde entier pour sa qualité. Elle a été conçue pour plaire aux petits et aux grands, et sa mission était d'attirer l'attention sur la fragilité de nos écosystèmes. Pentagram a souligné cette idée avec des ambiances spectaculaires qui mettaient en valeur la beauté individuelle de chacune des pièces exposées.

Questa mostra temporanea di meteoriti e fossili di dinosauri e animali estinti ha fatto registrare un'affluenza record di visitatori e ne è stata lodata la qualità su scala universale. Progettata per richiamare l'attenzione di grandi e piccini, tale esposizione mirava a evidenziare la fragilità dei nostri ecosistemi. Pentagram ha sottolineato quest'idea con un design volto a creare ambienti appassionanti, a risaltare la bellezza singola di ciascun pezzo in esposizione.

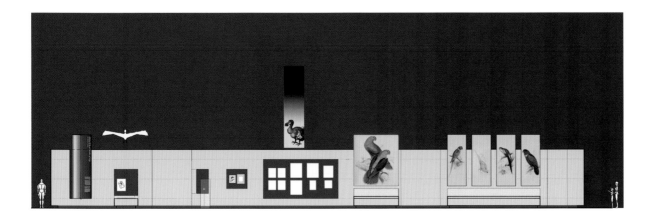

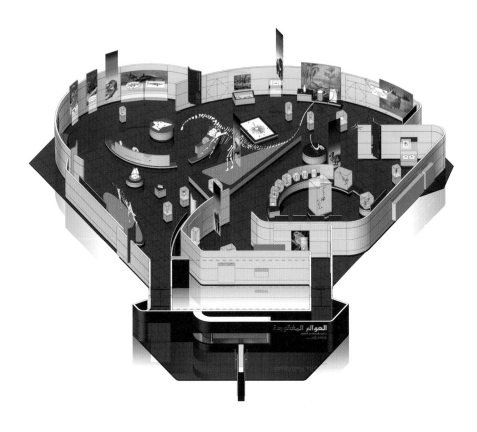

شهدت الأرض تغييرات كثيرة عبر تاريخها الطويل. فبينما ابتعدت قارات بأكملها عن بعضها البعض، التحمت قارات أخرى وغمرت بحار دافئة الأرض ثم تراجعت مخلفة وراءها صحارى مالحة. واستمرت الحياة بالتغير نتيجة هذه الأحداث الجسام.

منذ ملايين السنين، نمت أنواع جديدة من النباتات في الهواء الطلق مما شجع الكائنات الأولى على مغادرة البحار وتحولت السرخسيات إلى أشجار طويلة تسكن المستنقعات الدافئة. وبدأت الديناصورات والكائنات العملاقة الغريبة الأخرى تتغذى عليها. وعلى مر الزمن، سادت النباتات المزهرة عالم النبات. وحلت الطيور والثدييات مكان الديناصورات. أما اليوم، فقد انقرضت الكائنات العملاقة تاركة وراءها بقايا رائعة نشهد عليها.

The land has seen many changes over the history of this planet. Whole continents have drifted apart or clashed together. Warm seas have flooded the land, than retreated to leave salty deserts. Life has continually changed in response to these dramatic events.

Hundreds of millions of years ago, new types of plant grew in the open air. This encouraged the first creatures to leave the safety of the seas to feed along the shorelines of seas and lakes. Ferns grew into tall trees in warm swamps, and dinosaurs and other curious giants began to feed on them.

Over time, flowering plants came to dominate the plant world, and birds and mammals took the place of dinosaurs. Today, the giants have vanished, but they have left us spectacular remains.

Pentagram | London
Sonance Exhibit, Cedia Expo
Denver, CO, USA | 2006

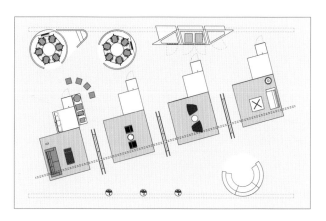

The brand Sonance offer top-of-the-range loudspeakers usually in combination with spectacular designer interiors. Consequently, the space conceived by Pentagram for this exhibition was bound to be attractive. This goal was achieved with the construction of a 3D structure of superimposed cubes in an almost impossible interplay of interconnected planes and vertices. This configuration recalls the journey of sound offered by the brand's equipment.

Die Marke Sonance bietet Luxus-Lautsprecher für außergewöhnliche Räume an. Daher sollte auch der Raum, den Pentagram für diese Ausstellung konzipierte, höchste Attraktivität besitzen. Dieses Ziel erreichte man mit der Konstruktion einer dreidimensionalen Struktur aus übereinander gelagerten Kuben, in einem fast unmöglichen Spiel aus untereinander verbundenen Horizontalen und Vertikalen. Dieses Gebilde lässt an die Schallwellen denken, wie sie die Anlagen der Marke produzieren.

La marca Sonance ofrece altavoces de lujo que suelen combinarse con interiores de diseño espectacular. Por este motivo, el espacio concebido por Pentagram para esta muestra debía resultar muy atractivo. Este objetivo se logró con la construcción de una estructura tridimensional de cubos superpuestos, que crea un juego casi imposible de vértices interconectados. Esta configuración evoca el recorrido del sonido que brindan los equipos de la marca.

La marque Sonance propose des enceintes audio de luxe qui trouvent leur place dans des intérieurs à la décoration spectaculaire. Pentagram devait donc concevoir pour cette exposition un espace vraiment superbe. L'agence s'est acquittée de cette tâche en construisant une structure tridimensionnelle de cubes superposés en un jeu presque impossible d'angles interconnectés. Cette installation évoque la trajectoire des sons qui sortent des produits de la marque.

La marca Sonance produce casse di lusso abbinate, in genere, a un favolosa architettura d'interni. L'obiettivo della Pentagram di creare uno spazio particolarmente allettante, come non poteva essere altrimenti, per questa mostra è stato raggiunto mediante la costruzione di una struttura tridimensionale di cubi sovrapposti, in un gioco quasi impossibile di piani e vertici interconnessi. Tale configurazione rievoca il percorso del suono emesso dalle apparecchiature della marca in oggetto.

THE SONANCE STORY

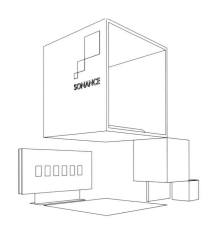

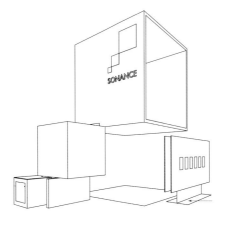

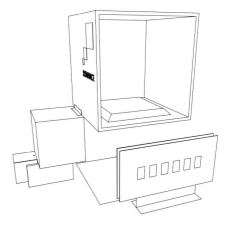

INVISIBLE   NEARLY INVISIBLE

Plajer & Franz Studio | Berlin
A3, Expo Real
Munich, Germany | 2007

The stand designed to promote the image of the holding company A3 stands out above all for its striking corporate colors. In line with the brand's philosophy, green evokes a business spirit, blue is for innovation, red stands for service provision and pink for lifestyle. The bands of color are mixed throughout the floor and walls and spread in the direction of the computer terminals and sales stands.

Der Stand zur Verbreitung des Images der Unternehmensholding A3 ragt vor allem dadurch heraus, dass die Farben der Corporate Identity sehr wirkungsvoll eingesetzt sind. Gemäß der Firmenphilosophie evoziert das Grün Unternehmensgeist, das Blau Innovation, das Rot Dienstleistungen und das Rosa Lifestyle. Die Farbstreifen mischen sich auf der gesamten Länge des Bodens und an den Wänden und entfalten sich in Richtung der Infoterminals und dorthin, wo man die Aussteller antrifft.

El stand diseñado para difundir la imagen del holding empresarial A3 llama la atención por lo impactante de los colores corporativos. Según la filosofía de la marca, el verde evoca el espíritu empresarial; el azul, la innovación; el rojo, la prestación de servicios, y el rosa, el estilo de vida. Las bandas de colores se entrecruzan a lo largo del suelo y las paredes, y se despliegan en dirección a los terminales informativos y los expositores.

Le stand conçu pour représenter la holding A3 se distingue par les couleurs vives de l'entreprise. Selon la philosophie de la marque, le vert évoque l'esprit d'entreprise, le bleu l'innovation, le rouge la prestation de services et le rose le style de vie. Les bandes de couleur s'entrecroisent tout le long du sol et des murs, et se déploient vers les terminaux d'information et les exposants.

Lo stand progettato per divulgare l'immagine dell'holding aziendale A3, spicca, grazie alla cromia corporativa di grande effetto. Secondo la filosofia della marca, il verde rievoca lo spirito aziendale, il blu l'innovazione, il rosso la prestazione di servizi e, il rosa, lo stile di vita. Le fasce colorate si mescolano lungo tutto il pavimento e sulle pareti e si svolgono verso i terminal informativi e gli espositori.

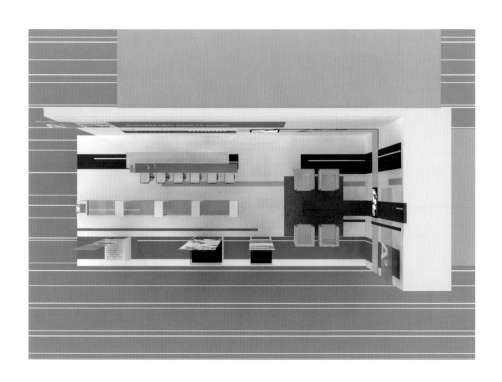

BUSINESS NEXT DOOR TO MUNICH

BESUCHER

Plajer & Franz Studio | Berlin
BMW Pavilion, International Automobile Exhibition
Berlin, Germany | 2005

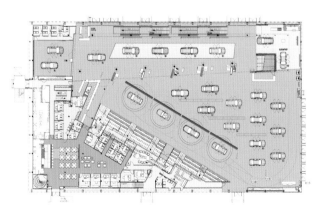

The world's biggest car show was home to this spectacular BMW display which involved developing a new way of conceiving the design of an exhibition site. The enormous pavilion covered a total area of 36,000 square feet and was covered in 166 airbags — an amazing effect from the outside, particularly given it could be disassembled in seven days.

Für diese spektakuläre Präsentierung der Firma BMW im Rahmen des weltweit größten Autosalons wurde eine neue Form für die Gestaltung von Ausstellungsflächen entwickelt. Der riesige Pavillon mit einer Gesamtfläche von 3370 Quadratmetern ist mit 166 Luftkissen bedeckt, wodurch die Außenansicht ungeheuer beeindruckend wirkt, vor allem, wenn man bedenkt, dass die Installation in sieben Tagen demontiert werden kann.

El salón del automóvil más grande del mundo acogió esta espectacular muestra de la firma BMW, para la que gestó una nueva forma de concebir el diseño de recintos de exhibición. El enorme pabellón, con un área de 3.370 m², está recubierto con 166 cojines de aire que le otorgan un aspecto exterior impactante, sobre todo teniendo en cuenta que la instalación se desmontó en tan sólo siete días.

C'est le plus grand salon de l'automobile du monde qui a accueilli cette exposition spectaculaire de la marque BMW, pour laquelle on a inventé une nouvelle façon de concevoir les espaces d'exposition. L'énorme pavillon, avec une surface totale de 3 370 m², a été recouvert de 166 coussins d'air qui lui ont donné un aspect extérieur des plus spectaculaires, surtout lorsqu'on sait que l'installation a été démontée en sept jours.

Il salone dell'automobile più grande del mondo ha ospitato questa spettacolare esposizione dell'azienda BMW, per la quale è stata concepita una nuova forma d'intendere la progettazione di spazi espositivi. Si è provveduto a ricoprire il grande padiglione, dalla superficie complessiva di 3.370 m², con 166 cuscini d'aria creando, così, un aspetto esterno di grande impatto, tenuto conto soprattutto del fatto che si è riusciti a smontare tale struttura in soli sette giorni.

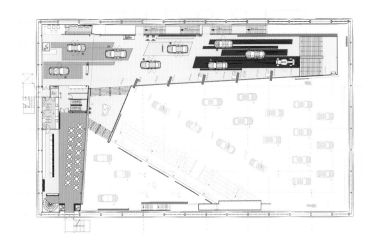
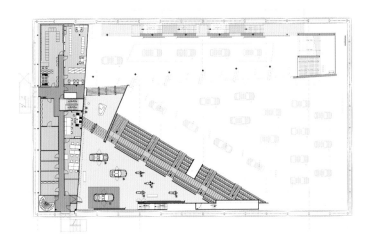

Die exklusivste Art, BMW zu fahren.
The most exclusive way of driving BMW.

BMW Individual

Plajer & Franz Studio | Berlin
Most Showroom, International Candy & Chocolate Exhibition
Cologne, Germany | 2006

Chocolate company Most, on the market for over 150 years, asked the studio to design a stand that would create a contemporary image while maintaining the brand's traditional nature. In just 130 square feet, Plajer & Franz Studio created a room charged with sensuality, one highlight of which is the eye-catching divan visitors are invited to sit on to sample the company's products. The well-furnished ambience, with art deco touches, speaks to luxury and seduction.

Die seit über 150 Jahren bestehende Schokoladenfirma Most beauftragte das Büro mit einem Stand, der ein modernes Image schaffen sollte, ohne den traditionellen Charakter der Marke zu vernachlässigen. Auf einer Fläche von gerade zwölf Quadratmetern schufen Plajer & Franz Studio einen Raum voller Sinnlichkeit, in dem ein auffälliger Diwan den Besucher einlädt, die Produkte des Hauses zu testen. Das überladene Ambiente mit Jugendstil-Reminiszenzen ruft ein Gefühl von Luxus und Verlockung wach.

La firma chocolatera Most, con más de 150 años de actividad, encargó al estudio un *stand* que creara una imagen contemporánea sin dejar de atender al carácter tradicional de la marca. En un espacio de tan sólo 12 m², Plajer & Franz Studio creó una sala cargada de sensualidad, en la que destaca un llamativo diván donde se invita al visitante a degustar los productos de la casa. El recargado ambiente, con reminiscencias del *art déco*, evoca lujo y seducción.

La marque de chocolat Most, qui existe depuis plus de 150 ans, a commandé au studio un stand capable de lui donner une image moderne sans faire oublier son caractère traditionnel. Dans un espace de seulement 12 m², Plajer & Franz Studio a créé une pièce baignée de sensualité. On y invite les visiteurs à déguster les produits de la maison sur un divan irrésistible. L'atmosphère chargée, d'inspiration art déco, évoque le luxe et la séduction.

La fabbrica di cioccolato Most, attiva da oltre 150 anni, ha incaricato lo studio di realizzare uno *stand* volto a dare un'immagine moderna, senza tralasciare il carattere tradizionale del marchio. In uno spazio di soli 12 m², lo studio Plajer & Franz Studio ha allestito una sala carica di sensualità con un vistoso sofà su cui il visitatore può comodamente degustare i prodotti della casa. Il fastoso ambiente, con reminiscenze *art décoratif*, evoca lusso e seduzione.

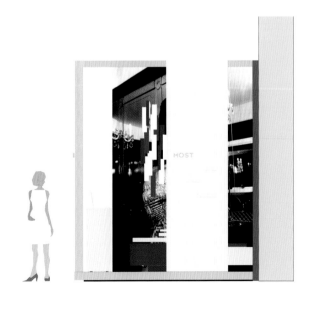

Plajer & Franz Studio | Berlin
Sixt, International Trade Fair for Tourism
Berlin, Germany | 2006

The leading German car-hire and leasing firm, with more than 3,500 offices, awarded Plajer & Franz Studio the job of promoting its business at this trade fair. The client required a space divided into four zones: reservation counter, meeting area or café, offices and information stand. With this premise, the studio designed the principal visual feature of the project: an orange dividing panel which can be folded up to convert into a ceiling.

Die deutsche Firma mit Schwerpunkt im Bereich Leihwagen- und Leasing-Fahrzeuge beauftragte Plajer & Franz Studio damit, auf dieser Messe über ihr Arbeitsspektrum mit über 3500 Filialen zu informieren. Der Kunde wünschte eine Aufteilung in vier Bereiche: Schaufenster der Auto-Reservierung, Meeting Point oder Cafeteria, Büros und Informationsstand. Unter diesen Voraussetzungen wurde der in ein Dach übergehende Raumteiler aus orangen Paneelen entworfen, das wichtigste visuelle Aushängeschild des Projekts.

La firma alemana con mayor actividad en coches de alquiler y leasing, y con más de 3.500 sucursales, encomendó a Plajer & Franz Studio la tarea de divulgar en esta feria su amplia labor. El cliente requería cuatro espacios diferenciados: un mostrador para las reservas, un área de reunión o cafetería, oficinas y un puesto informativo. Con estas premisas, se concibió el elemento divisorio del panel naranja, que se dobla para convertirse en techo, principal reclamo visual del proyecto.

Pour ce salon, la société allemande la plus active dans le domaine de la location et du leasing de voitures a chargé Plajer & Franz Studio de représenter ses vastes activités, avec plus de 3 500 succursales. Le client voulait quatre espaces : un comptoir de réservation, un espace de réunion, des bureaux et un poste d'information. C'est dans cet esprit qu'a été conçu le panneau de division orange, qui se plie pour former un toit et constitue le principal élément visuel du projet.

La società tedesca più attiva nel settore dell'autonoleggio e leasing ha affidato allo studio Plajer & Franz Studio il compito di divulgare, in questa fiera, la sua vasta attività di oltre 3.500 filiali. Il committente aveva richiesto una suddivisione in quattro zone: banco prenotazioni, area riunioni o caffè, uffici e postazione informativa. Così è stato eretto l'elemento divisorio del pannello arancione, pieghevole con funzione di copertura, principale reclamo visivo del progetto.

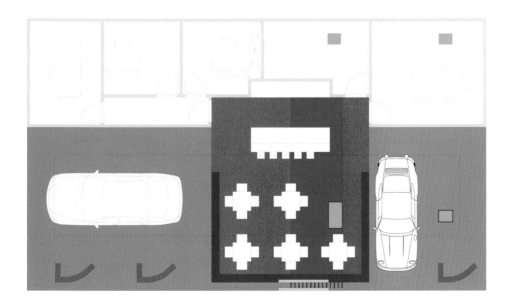

Quinze & Milan | Kortrijk
Caged Beauty, Interieur Biennale
Kortrijk, Belgium | 2006

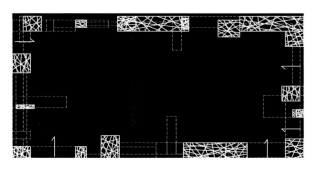

For the Moroso showroom at the International Interior Biennial in Kortrijk, Arne Quinze had the firm idea of creating a transparent and accessible cabin, positioning each design on a pedestal in honor of its inventor. The result was a spectacular sculpture built from fiberglass boxes. The forms of the grid bring to mind spider webs. Above it is the spectacular white lighting, which both frames and highlights the colorful material on display.

Für den Showroom der Marke Moroso bei der Intérieur, Biennale für Innenarchitektur, im belgischen Kortirjk hatte Arne Quinze die klare Absicht, eine durchsichtige und zugängliche Kabine zu schaffen und jeden Designentwurf auf einem Sockel zu Ehren des jeweiligen Urhebers zu platzieren. Das Ergebnis war eine spektakuläre Skulptur mit Kästen aus Fieberglas. Die Formen des Rasters lassen an ein Spinnennetz denken, auf das die Beleuchtung in atemberaubender Weise fällt. Das Weiß rahmt die farbigen Ausstellungsmaterialien und hebt sie hervor.

Para el salón de exposiciones de Moroso, en la Bienal internacional de diseño de interiores celebrada en Kortrijk, Arne Quinze tenía la firme intención de crear una cabina transparente y accesible, distribuyendo cada diseño en un pedestal en honor de su artífice. El resultado es una espectacular escultura construida con cajas de fibra de vidrio. Las formas de la cuadrícula evocan telas de araña. Sobre ella incide una iluminación espectacular; el blanco enmarca y resalta el colorido del material expuesto.

Pour le showroom de Morosa à la Biennale internationale de l'intérieur de Kortrijk, Arne Quinze a eu l'idée de créer une cabine transparente et accessible. Chaque concept est posé sur un piédestal pour rendre hommage à son inventeur.Le résultat est une sculpture spectaculaire faite de boîtes en fibre de verre. Les formes du quadrillage évoquent des toiles d'araignée. La lumière y crée des effets spectaculaires, et le blanc encadre et souligne les couleurs des pièces exposées.

Per la showroom di Moroso presso la Biennale internazionale di design d'interni a Kortrijk, Arne Quinze era fermamente intenzionata a creare una cabina trasparente e accessibile, disponendone ogni singolo design su un piedistallo in onore del suo artefice. Il risultato è una scultura spettacolare fatta di scatole di fibra di vetro. Le forme della quadrettatura rievocano le ragnatele. Tale scultura viene evidenziata da un'illuminazione spettacolare di cui il colore bianco incornicia e mette in risalto il colore del materiale ivi esposto.

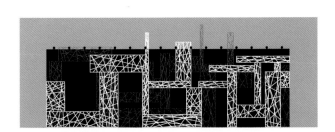

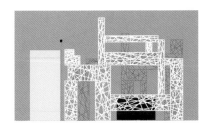

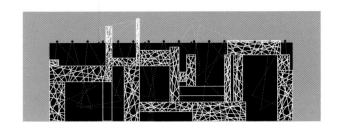

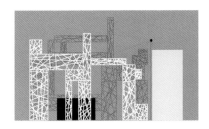

The Experience Lab-

Quinze & Milan | Kortrijk
Jaga Showroom, Superstudio Più
Milan, Italy | 2006

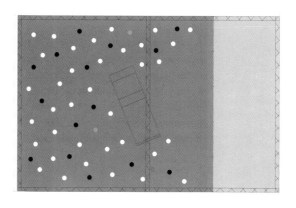

This stand aimed to promote the new brand of Iguana radiators. The pillars that sustain the stand reproduce the shape of the radiators, creating a play of colors through a simple use of black and white. With a sporadic touch of green that represents nature, the pillars surround an interior space that aimed to reflect a bedroom where visitors could perceive the warmth provided by the radiators.

Dieser Stand bezweckt, die neue Radiator-Marke Iguana bekannt zu machen. Die Pfeiler, die den Stand halten, nehmen die Form der Radiatoren auf und bringen durch den einfachen Einsatz von Weiß und Schwarz ein Farbspiel hervor. Hier und da mit einem Hauch von Grün, welches das Element der Natur verkörpert, markieren diese Pfeiler einen Innenraum, der wie ein Zimmer wirkt, in dem man die Wärme wahrnehmen kann, welche die Radiatoren verbreiten.

Este *stand* tiene como propósito dar a conocer la nueva marca de radiadores Iguana. Los pilares que sostienen el *stand* reproducen la forma de los radiadores y crean un juego de colores con el uso del blanco y el negro. Con algunos toques de verde, color que representa la naturaleza, estos pilares rodean un espacio interior que pretende ser el reflejo de una habitación, en la que los visitantes puedan percibir la calidez proporcionada por los radiadores.

Ce *stand* a pour objectif de faire connaître et de positionner la nouvelle marque de radiateurs Iguana. Les piliers qui soutiennent le stand reproduisent la forme de ces radiateurs, et créent un jeu chromatique simple entre le blanc et le noir. Agrémentés de quelques touches de vert, couleur qui représente l'élément naturel, ces piliers encadrent un espace intérieur qui veut évoquer la pièce d'un logement où l'on peut percevoir la chaleur des radiateurs.

Questo *stand* si prefigge di far conoscere la nuova marca di termosifoni Iguana. I pilastri sostenenti lo stand, richiamano la forma dei termosifoni e creano un gioco di colori utilizzando semplicemente il bianco e il nero. Con uno sprazzo di verde raffigurante la natura, questi pilastri racchiudono uno spazio interno come se fosse una grande stanza, in cui è percepibile il calore fornito dai termosifoni.

CONCEPT BY
ARNE QUINZE
FOR JAGA.BE

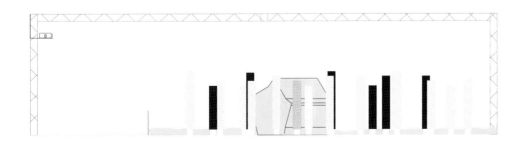

Quinze & Milan | Kortrijk
Mutagenesis, Abitare il Tempo
Verona, Italy | 2007

What has always set **Abitare il Tempo** apart from other exhibitions is its ability to promote exhibitions that incorporate progress into the field of design. Mutagenesis is the term used in genetics for the production of mutations in DNA, whether cloned or not, and is the theme that inspired the designer to create a space where sculptures interact like mutagens. The exhibition is structured around two pillars: Artifacts of Today and Artifacts of the Future.

Was die Messe Abitare il Tempo von anderen Ausstellungen unterscheidet, ist ihre Fähigkeit, Ausstellungen zu fördern, die Fortschritt im Bereich Design miteinbeziehen. In der Genetik nennt man Mutagenese die Erzeugung von Veränderungen der DNA, unabhängig von Klonung. Diese Thematik, inspirierte den Designer, einen Raum zu realisieren, in dem die Skulpturen wie Mutagene interagieren. Die Ausstellung ist um zwei thematische Säulen angelegt: Artefakte heute und Artefakte morgen.

Lo que diferencia Abitare il Tempo de otras exposiciones siempre ha sido su capacidad para promover exposiciones que resuman la evolución en el campo del diseño. En genética, se denomina mutagénesis a la producción de mutaciones sobre ADN, clonado o no. Éste es el tema que ha inspirado al diseñador para realizar un espacio en donde las esculturas interactúan como mutágenos. La muestra se estructura en torno a dos pilares: Artefactos de hoy y Artefactos del futuro.

Ce qui a toujours distingué Abitare il Tempo des autres salons est sa capacité à proposer des expositions qui résument les évolutions dans le domaine du design. La mutagenèse est la production de mutations sur l'ADN, qu'il soit cloné ou non, et c'est ce thème qui a inspiré le designer dans la création de cet espace où les sculptures interagissent comme des mutagènes. L'exposition est organisée autour de deux piliers : Artefacts d'aujour'hui et Artefacts du futur.

A differenziare Abitare il Tempo da altre mostre è sempre stata la sua capacità di promuovere esposizioni sintetizzanti l'evoluzione nel campo della progettazione. In genetica, con il termine mutagenesi si definisce il processo di mutazione del DNA, clonato o meno. È questo l'argomento cui si è ispirato il designer per realizzare uno spazio ove le sculture interagiscono come mutageni. La mostra si svolge attorno a due pilastri: Aggeggi odierni e Aggeggi futuri.

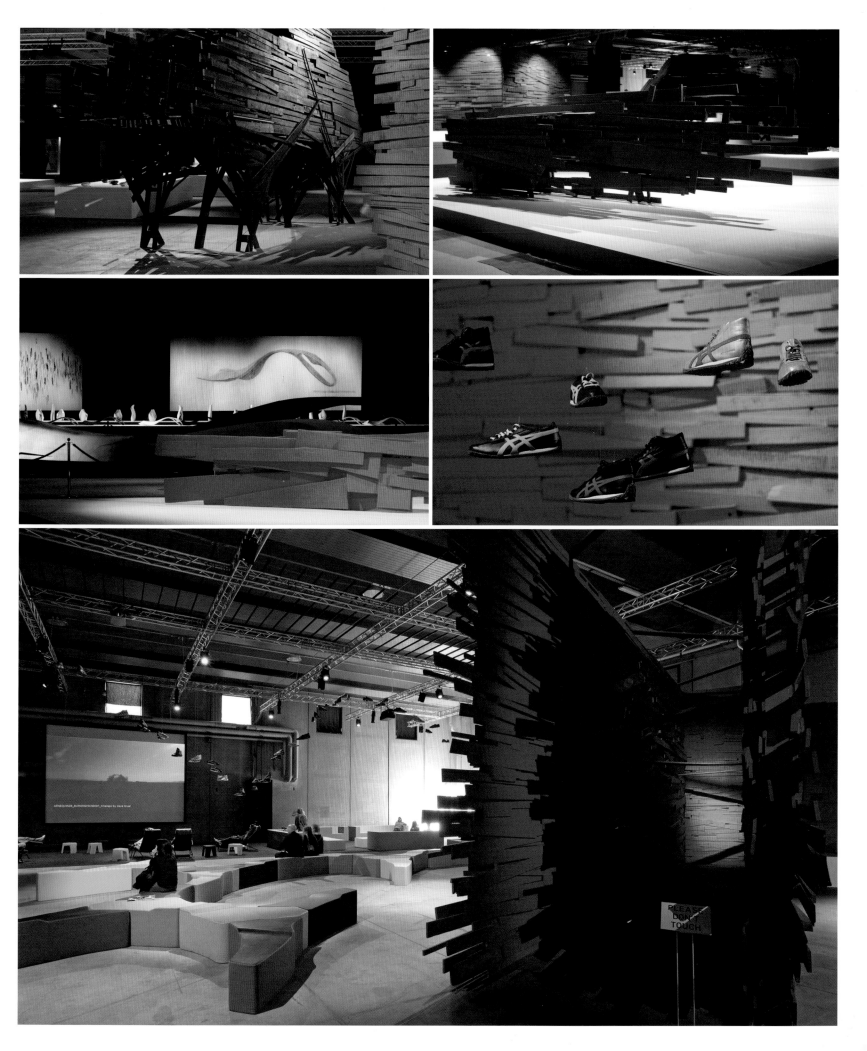

Quinze & Milan | Kortrijk
Club, Design Post
Cologne, Germany | 2006

The design by Q & M for Design Post offers an exciting exhibition space that encompasses a total of 20 zones used throughout the year by internationally renowned design companies. Arne Quinze developed a wooden structure on one of the mezzanine levels. The installation interacts with the functionality of the old corrugated steel sheet in which it is located. In total, the construction required six miles of wood, 50,000 nails and 18 boxes of polyester.

Die Gestaltung, die Q & M für die Design Post entwickelte, bietet eine mitreißende Ausstellungsräumlichkeit, die insgesamt 20 Bereiche umfasst, die das Jahr über von international renommierten Designfirmen bespielt werden. Arne Quinze konzipierte eine Holzstruktur in einem der Zwischenstockwerke. Die Installation steht in Wechselwirkung mit der Funktionalität der alten Stahlplatte, auf der sie platziert ist. Insgesamt wurden für die Konstruktion zehn Kilometer Holz, 50.000 Nägel und 18 Kisten Polyester verbraucht.

El diseño realizado por Q & M, a partir de un encargo de la sociedad Design Post, ha previsto un espacio expositivo de indudable interés, compuesto en total por veinte zonas utilizadas durante todo el año por sociedades de diseño de fama internacional. Arne Quinze ha concebido una estructura de madera en una de las entreplantas. Esta instalación interactúa con la funcionalidad de la antigua hoja de acero corrugado en la que está ubicada. En total, la construcción requirió de 10 km de madera, cincuenta mil clavos y dieciocho cajas de poliéster.

Le concept que Q & M a réalisé pour Design Post est un espace d'exposition très intéressant. Il comprend un total de 20 zones que des sociétés de design de renom international utilisent tout au long de l'année. Arne Quinze a imaginé une structure en bois sur l'une des mezzanines. L'installation interagit avec la fonctionnalité de la feuille d'acier ondulé sur laquelle elle a été placée. Sa construction a nécessité un total de 10 kilomètres de bois, 50 000 clous et 18 caisses de polyester.

Il design eseguito da Q & M per conto della società Design Post, ha previsto uno spazio espositivo di indubbio interesse, comprendente complessivamente 20 zone impiegate in tutto l'arco dell'anno da società di design di chiara fama internazionale. Arne Quinze ha concepito una struttura lignea su uno dei soppalchi. Tale struttura interagisce con la funzionalità della vecchia lamina di acciaio corrugato in cui è ubicata. Nel complesso, la costruzione ha richiesto l'uso di una quantità di legno lunga 10 km, 50.000 chiodi e 18 scatole in poliestere.

RCR Arquitectes | Girona
Hammershoi on the Light of Dreyer, CCCB
Barcelona, Spain | 2007

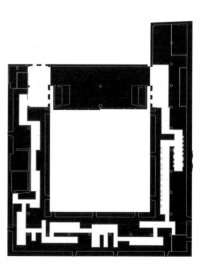

With the goal of understanding the relationship between Hammershoi's paintings and Dreyer's films, the leitmotif of this exhibition was the treatment of light, a prominent feature in the works of both artists. Here the lighting in the installation does not illuminate the painting but rather enables the painting to illuminate the space, and at times is limited to the light provided by candles — giving visitors a feeling of stillness and austerity.

Mit dem Ziel, die Beziehung zwischen den Gemälden von Hammershoi und den Filmen Dreyers zu verstehen, ist das Leitmotiv dieser Ausstellung, der Umgang mit Licht, der in den Werken beider Künstler so wichtig ist. Hier illuminiert das Licht der Installation nicht die Malerei, sondern erlaubt es umgekehrt, dass die Malerei den Raum beleuchtet; hier und da beschränkt man sich auf Kerzen, um dem Besucher das Gefühl von Ruhe und Schlichtheit zu vermitteln.

Con el objetivo de entender la relación entre las producciones pictóricas de Hammershoi y los trabajos cinematográficos de Dreyer, esta exposición tiene como leitmotif el tratamiento de la luz, tan importante en las obras de ambos creadores. En esta muestra, la luz no ilumina las pinturas, sino que deja que sean éstas las que iluminen el espacio. A veces la luz se limita tan sólo a la de unas velas, para despertar en el visitante quietud y austeridad.

Cette exposition explore la relation entre les peintures d'Hammershoi et les films de Dreyer, et son leitmotiv est le traitement de la lumière, qui joue un rôle de premier plan dans l'œuvre des deux artistes. La lumière de l'installation n'éclaire pas la peinture, au contraire elle laisse à la peinture le soin d'illuminer l'espace, et se limite parfois à quelques bougies afin d'inspirer aux visiteurs des notions de tranquillité et d'austérité.

Per rendere comprensibili i rapporti tra le produzioni pittoriche di Hammershoi e quelle cinematografiche di Dreyer, il leitmotif di questa mostra è l'importante uso della luce nelle opere di entrambi i creatori. In questo caso, la luce dell'allestimento non illumina la pittura bensì consente alla pittura di illuminare lo spazio. Talvolta, per destare nel visitatore sensazioni di quiete e austerità, si fa ricorso soltanto alla luce emessa da qualche candela.

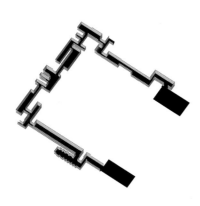 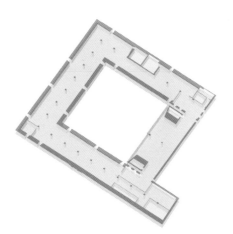 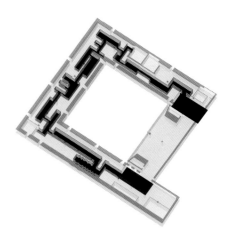

Ronan & Erwan Bouroullec | Paris
La Pelota Installation, La Pelota Sports Center
Milan, Italy | 2005

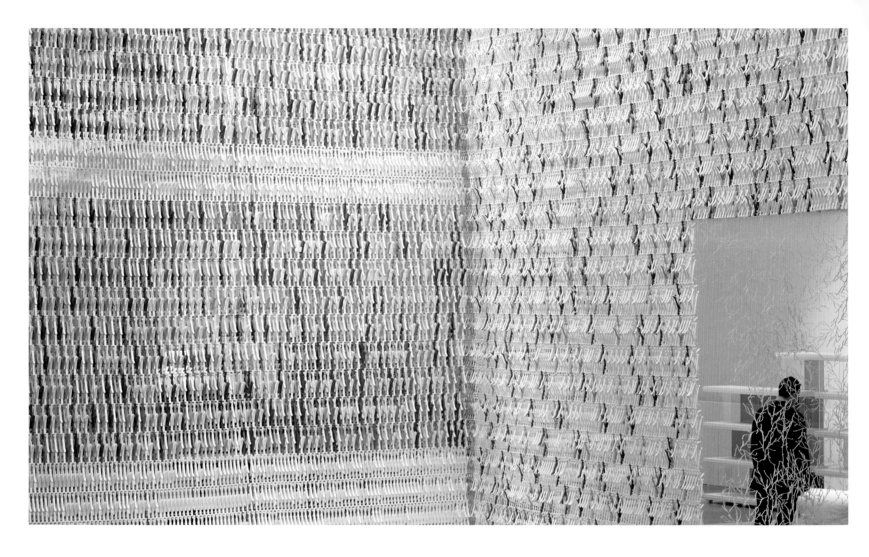

The Bouroullec brothers' original idea, i.e., to divide large spaces into a series of smaller, differently shaped exhibition areas, was achieved thanks to a system based on using a textile material that provided good acoustic insulation and guaranteed separation into comfortable areas for visitors. The simplicity of the structure was compensated for by the chromatic possibilities.

Die ursprüngliche Idee der Gebrüder Bouroullec, die darin bestand, große Räume in eine Reihe von kleineren Ausstellungsbereichen mit verschiedenen Formen zu unterteilen, gelingt bei diesem Projekt dank eines Systems, das auf dem Einsatz von textilem Material beruht. Dadurch wird eine gute Schalldämmung erreicht und bequeme Bereiche für die Besucher geschaffen. Die anfängliche Einfachheit der Struktur wird kompensiert durch die Möglichkeiten ihrer Farbgestaltung.

La idea original de los hermanos Bouroullec —dividir grandes espacios para convertirlos en zonas de exposición de menor tamaño con formas diferentes— se materializa en este proyecto gracias a un sistema basado en el uso de un material textil que ofrece un buen aislamiento acústico y garantiza la separación en áreas cómodas para los visitantes de las exposiciones. La sencillez de la estructura se compensa con sus posibilidades cromáticas.

L'idée originale des frères Bouroullec —diviser de grands espaces pour les convertir en une série de zones d'exposition de plus petite taille et de différentes formes— se concrétise dans ce projet grâce à un système basé sur l'utilisation d'un textile qui a la propriété d'être un bon isolant acoustique et qui divise l'espace en zones confortables pour les visiteurs des expositions. La simplicité de la structure est compensée par ses possibilités chromatiques.

L'idea originale dei fratelli Bouroullec —suddividere i grandi spazi per farne una serie di spazi espositivi più piccoli, con forme diverse— si materializza in questo progetto grazie a un sistema basato sull'uso di un materiale tessile che rende possibile un buon isolamento acustico e garantisce la separazione in comode aree per i visitatori delle mostre. La semplicità della struttura viene controbilanciata dalle sue possibilità cromatiche.

1973

DÉSOLÉ, plus d'essence

SORRY, Out of Gas

Saucier & Perrotte Architectes | Paris
Sorry, Out of Gas, Canadian Centre for Architects (CCA)
Montréal, Canada | 2007-2008

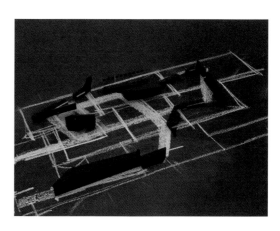

Designed by Canadian architect Gilles Saucier from Saucier & Perrotte Architectes, the exhibition makes use of an imposing dark-toned structure to link together the different galleries and establish a continuous route around the diverse spaces. Visitors can penetrate the gallery walls or submerge themselves in the common evaluation system of various archives. The graphic design is the work of Zab Design & Typography from Winnipeg, Canada.

Diese Ausstellungsarchitektur von dem kanadischen Architekten Gilles Saucier von Saucier & Perrotte Architectes konzipiert, besteht aus impulsanten dunkelfarbigen Elementen, die die einzelnen Galerien miteinander verbinden und somit einen fließenden Rundgang durch alle Räumlichkeiten erzeugen. Der Besucher dringt durch die Wände der Galerie und taucht in das allgemeine Evaluierungssystem mit verschiedenen Archiven ein. Die grafische Umsetzung wurde von Zab Design & Typography aus dem kanadischen Winnipeg realisiert.

Diseñada por el arquitecto canadiense Gilles Saucier de Saucier & Perrotte Architectes, la exposición se compone de una imponente estructura de tonos oscuros que enlaza las galerías y establece un recorrido continuo por los diversos espacios. El visitante penetra a través de las paredes de la galería y se sumerge en el sistema de evaluación común de varios archivos. El diseño gráfico ha sido realizado por Zab Design & Typography, de Winnipeg, Canadá.

Cette exposition conçue par l'architecte canadien Gilles Saucier, de Saucier & Perrotte Architectes, se compose d'une imposante structure de couleurs sombres qui relie les différentes galeries et trace un parcours continu à travers les espaces. Les visiteurs pénètrent à travers les murs de la galerie et s'immergent dans le système d'évaluation commun de plusieurs archives. Le graphisme est l'œuvre de Zab Design & Typography, une agence de Winnipeg, au Canada.

Progettata dall'architetto canadese Gilles Saucier dello studio Saucier & Perrotte Architectes, tale mostra si avvale di un'imponente struttura dalle tonalità scure che mette in comunicazione le varie gallerie e definisce un percorso continuo nei vari spazi. Il visitatore attraversa le pareti della galleria per tuffarsi nel sistema di valutazione comune di vari archivi. Veste grafica a cura di Zab Design & Typography, di Winnipeg, Canada.

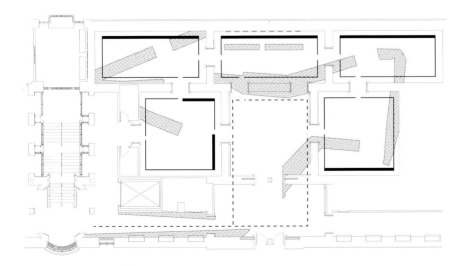

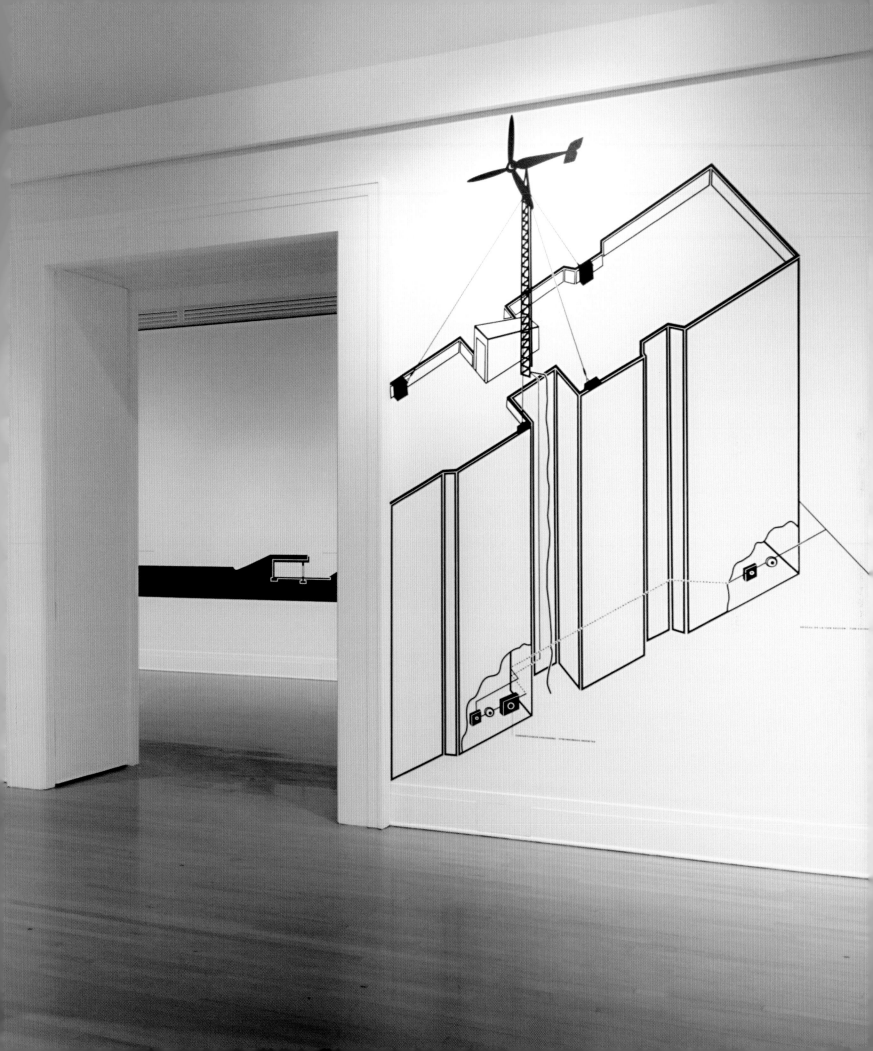

Designed as if it were a majestic temple, the complete space of this pavilion covers 2,100 square feet. The elongated shape of the pavilion looks elegant and modest at the same time. This 'nomadic' construction can be considered an environmentally friendly design piece. In this case, the pavilion was used to display chairs designed by Artek, but it can also be otherwise employed as a meeting point for the trademark's professional community.

Die Gesamtfläche dieses Pavillons in der Art eines majestätischen Tempels beträgt 200 Quadratmeter. Seine längliche Form verleiht ihm einen eleganten und zugleich bescheidenen Ausdruck. Diese „nomadische" Konstruktion kann man als ökologisches Designerstück bezeichnen. Im konkreten Fall wurde der Pavillon als Ausstellungsort für Designer-Stühle von Artek benutzt, aber man kann ihn ebenso als Treffpunkt einsetzen für diejenigen, die beruflich mit dieser Marke zu tun haben.

Diseñado como si se tratara de un templo majestuoso, el espacio completo de este pabellón ocupa 200 m². La forma alargada del pabellón le otorga un aspecto elegante y modesto al mismo tiempo. Esta construcción «nómada» puede considerarse una pieza de diseño ecológico. En este caso, se empleó el pabellón como lugar de exposición de las sillas diseñadas por Artek, pero también actúa como punto de encuentro para la comunidad profesional de la marca comercial.

Ce pavillon de 200 m² a été conçu comme un temple majestueux. Sa forme allongée lui donne une apparence élégante et modeste à la fois. Cette structure « nomade » peut être qualifiée d'exemple de design écologique. Ici, le pavillon accueille une exposition de chaises créées par Artek, mais il peut aussi servir de point de rencontre pour la communauté professionnelle de la marque commerciale.

Progettato come se fosse un tempio maestoso, lo spazio di questo padiglione misura complessivamente 200 m². La forma allungata del padiglione gli conferisce un'aria elegante e modesta nel contempo. Tale costruzione «nomade» può considerarsi un pezzo di design ecologico. In questo caso, il padiglione ha avuto la funzione di luogo d'esposizione delle sedie progettate Artek, benché sia utilizzabile anche come punto di raduno per gli addetti ai lavori della marca commerciale.

DAY LIVING

EL CAMÍ CAP A LES ELECCIONS DEL 15 DE JUNY

...embres del govern d'UCD ...laudeixen l'aprovació de la Llei ...mnistia. Madrid, 14 d'octubre

el desembre ...e 1976, la Llei de Reforma Política per ...6,5 milions de vots afirmatius sobre ...n cens de 22,6 milions, l'atenció queda ...ixada a la capital de l'Estat. Estava ...n joc la realitat de l'evolució a ...a democràcia que volia impulsar ...el govern d'Adolfo Suárez.

El comte de Barcelona cedeix els seus drets dinàstics a favor del seu fill, el rei Joan Carles. Madrid, 14 de maig
Foto: EFE

...egalització del *Partido Comunista* ...e España (PCE). Madrid, 9 d'abril

Legalització del *Partido Comunista de España* (PCE). Madrid, 9 d'abril
Al centre, Ramon Tamames i Ignacio Gallego

Silvia Farriol | Barcelona
Ja som aquí!, Palau Robert
Barcelona, Spain | 2007

Within the image:

JA SOM AQUÍ!
MEMÒRIA D'EFE

EFE: Catalunya   Generalitat de Catalunya

Per als pobles d'Espanya, el 1977 no va ser un any com els altres. Franco havia mort el 20 de novembre de 1975 i durant el segon semestre de 1976, el rei Joan Carles va escollir Adolfo Suárez com a nou president del govern. Suárez, amb l'ajuda del president de les Corts Torcuato Fernández Miranda, va aconseguir la dissolució voluntària de les Corts franquistes i el desmantellament institucional de la dictadura. Al carrer, l'oposició democràtica i amplis segments socials pressionaven per una democratització real de les institucions i del país. Quedava obert el procés democràtic que conduiria a la convocatòria electoral del 15 de juny.

1977

This exhibition gathers together graphic material from the EFE news agency and other objects and documents related to the return of Catalan President Josep Tarradellas to Spain in 1977 after the end of the Franco era. The exhibition displays large vinyl murals, portraits of important people of the time covered in transparent methacrylate, a painting by Antoni Tàpies and even the convertible Lincoln Continental Tarradellas used upon his arrival.

In dieser Ausstellung wurden grafisches Material der Agentur EFE, andere Objekte und Dokumente zusammengetragen, die mit der Rückkehr des Präsidenten Tarradellas nach Spanien im Jahr 1977, nach dem Ende der Franco-Diktatur, zu tun haben. Zu sehen sind in der Präsentation große Vinyl-Wandbilder, Porträts wichtiger Persönlichkeiten der Epoche, ein Gemälde von Antoni Tàpies und der Lincoln Continental mit offenem Verdeck, den Tarradella bei seiner Ankunft in Spanien fuhr.

Esta exposición recopila material gráfico de la Agencia EFE y otros objetos y documentos relacionados con el regreso a España del presidente Tarradellas en 1977, tras el fin del franquismo. Se exhiben en la muestra grandes murales de vinilo, retratos de personajes importantes de la época cubiertos con metacrilato transparente, un cuadro de Antoni Tàpies y hasta el Lincoln Continental descapotable que Tarradellas empleó a su llegada.

Cette exposition rassemble des documents graphiques de l'Agence EFE et d'autres objets et documents liés au retour en Espagne du président Tarradellas en 1977, à la fin du franquisme. On y voit de grandes fresques en vinyle, des portraits de personnages importants de l'époque recouverts de méthacrylate transparent, un tableau d'Antoni Tàpies et même la décapotable Lincoln Continental que Tarradellas avait utilisée à son arrivée.

In tale mostra è esposto materiale grafico dell'Agenzia EFE nonché altri oggetti e documenti legati al ritorno in Spagna del presidente Tarradellas nel 1977, dopo il tramonto del franchismo. Vi si esibiscono murales di grandi proporzioni fatti di vinile, ritratti di personaggi di spicco dell'epoca, rivestiti di metacrilato trasparente, un quadro di Antoni Tàpies e persino una Lincoln Continental decappottabile di cui si servì Tarradellas al suo arrivo.

ment, portaran
lau de la Generalitat
ran velocitat: el 19
olea de Parlamentaris
i transitòria per
alitat; el 4 d'agost
ena els membres
gociadora amb
1 d'agost, a París,
ador Sánchez-Terán,
president Adolfo
ssos decisius en la
ca.

ONZE DE SETEMBRE.
DIADA NACIONAL
DE CATALUNYA

Una gran manifestació recorre el passeig de
Gràcia de Barcelona. El retorn de Tarradellas
com a president de la Generalitat és una de
les reivindicacions principals, juntament
amb l'amnistia per als presos polítics i
l'Estatut d'Autonomia.

Santiago Carrillo Solares
Gijón, 1915

Adolfo Suárez González
Cebreros, Ávila, 1932

Felipe González Márquez
Sevilla, 1942

Vicente Enrique y Tarancón
Borriana, Castelló de la Plana, 1907

Marcelino Camacho Abad
Osma La Rasa, Sòria, 1918

INDEX